GEOLOGICAL SURVEY OF CALIFORNIA.

J. D. WHITNEY, State Geologist.

CONTRIBUTIONS

TO

BAROMETRIC HYPSOMETRY:

WITH TABLES FOR USE

IN CALIFORNIA.

PUBLISHED BY AUTHORITY OF THE LEGISLATURE.

1874.

BAROMETRIC HYPSOMETRY.

GEOLOGICAL SURVEY OF CALIFORNIA.

J. D. WHITNEY, State Geologist.

CONTRIBUTIONS

TO

BAROMETRIC HYPSOMETRY:

WITH TABLES FOR USE

IN CALIFORNIA.

PUBLISHED BY AUTHORITY OF THE LEGISLATURE.

1874.

Universuty Press: Welch, Bigelow, & Co.,
Cambridge.

PREFATORY NOTE.

HAVING been, for more than twenty-five years, almost constantly employed in geological surveys of our Western States, I have had occasion to use the barometer quite extensively as a hypsometrical instrument. As early as 1847, being engaged in determining the height of points along the south shore of Lake Superior, I became convinced that there were sources of error in our barometrical work which had not been sufficiently taken into account; and by repeated measurements of a number of elevations at different seasons and hours, I arrived at the conclusion that our results were always lower in cold weather, or at morning and evening, than they were in warmer weather or towards noon. For some years after this my field of labor was among the prairies of the Mississippi Valley, where there was little occasion for hypsometrical work, and the subject of the uncertainties and perplexities of barometrical determinations of heights was for a time dismissed from my thoughts.

Later, however, on taking charge of the Geological Survey of California, where the barometer became again an instrument of the greatest importance, and indeed an indispensable companion in our field-work, the same difficulties which had been met with on Lake Superior began again to be noticed, and to call for investigation. Learning, however, that Colonel Williamson was engaged in making, under the authority of the United States Engineer Bureau, a series of observations with a view to the publication of an elaborate work on the use of the barometer as a hypsometrical instrument, it was deemed best to defer undertaking any researches of our own until after his had been completed, and the results printed. The Geological Survey, meanwhile, lent such aid to this distinguished officer as it was in our power to furnish. On the publication of his volume, however, it was found that, although thorough and valuable as far as it went, it did not fully meet our needs, but that the investigation required to be carried a little further, in order that results might be had which could be put to practical use.

The great expense of the determination by the spirit-level of the elevation of a number of points in the Sierra Nevada between its base and summit was an obstacle to our commencing the proposed work; but the completion of the Central Pacific Railroad seemed to remove this difficulty, by giving us not only pretty accurately the elevation desired, but also a chance for permanent stations and good observers among the telegraph operators employed at the different offices along the line. It was therefore decided that three points should be selected, and observations made three times a day at each, for a period of one year, and, if possible, for three, as is fully set forth in the second chapter of this little work. Here I must take occasion to return sincere thanks to Leland Stanford, President of the Central Pacific Railroad, for facilities furnished us during this series of observations; for, without his help, it would hardly have been possible for us to carry on the investigation.

A fourth station at an elevation of twelve thousand to fourteen thousand feet was very desirable; but this great enlargement of the plan was entirely beyond our means, and we were obliged to content ourselves with the summit station of the railroad as our highest point.

At the time this investigation was commenced I had very little acquaintance with anything which had been done by others in the direction of our own line of inquiry. It did not appear, however, that any such tables of correction as we hoped to prepare had ever come into practical use; and it became more and more evident, as our work went on, that, in all probability, our results would be of value to observers on the Pacific coast. Books of reference were not to be obtained there; but now that we have procured them, — and not without considerable search in Europe, — and know that others have gone over very nearly the same ground that we have, it appears none the less desirable that our investigations should have been made, or that they should now be published. Indeed, we have at present more confidence than ever in their value, although less entitled to claim merit for originality than we had supposed ourselves to be; for we now perceive very clearly that each country and climate demands something similar to that which we have attempted to do for California, if the hypsometric data obtained by the use of the barometer are to be rendered as accurate as possible, which every one will admit to be highly desirable. It is indeed probable that the Pacific coast is one of those regions where the barometric results are most liable to those discrepancies which have been the subject of our investigations, and that on this account our work has been particularly needed there; but it is clear that the uncertainties in question cannot anywhere be neglected, and that by the use of suitable tables of correction for the hour of the day and the season of the year, the accuracy of the barometer as a hypsometric instrument may be very considerably increased.

Professor W. H. Pettee, of Harvard University, has had charge of the onerous labor of the reduction and computation of the observations; and this little volume, prepared by him from the data collected by the Survey, owes a large share of its value to his accurate and persevering work upon it. With his assistance a very complete library of works devoted to the barometer ·has been accumulated, and in every case the references here given have been verified by consultation of the original authorities. It is believed that nothing of importance connected with the present inquiry can have escaped our notice, and that in the concluding chapter of this work a pretty complete *résumé* of the labors of other investigators has been presented.

J. D. W.

CAMBRIDGE, MASS., May 28, 1874.

TABLE OF CONTENTS.

CHAPTER I.

INTRODUCTORY.

CHAPTER II.

DETAILED ACCOUNT OF THE INVESTIGATION IN CALIFORNIA.

CHAPTER III.

RÉSUMÉ OF SIMILAR INVESTIGATIONS OUTSIDE OF CALIFORNIA.

SUPPLEMENTARY CHAPTER.

(ADDED 1878.)

A PRACTICAL APPLICATION OF THE TABLES TO THE OBSERVATIONS OF THE YEARS 1870-71, AND A DISCUSSION OF THE RESULTS OBTAINED.

CHAPTER I.

INTRODUCTORY.

THE main principle underlying the method of determining altitudes, or differences of altitude, by means of the barometer is simple, and easily understood. From the observed heights of the columns of mercury in two barometers at different altitudes, but not separated by any great distance horizontally, we have at once the weights of a column of air reaching from the lower instrument to the outer limit of the atmosphere, and of that portion of the air-column which rises above the upper instrument. The weight of the column of air between the two instruments is therefore known; and it would seem at first sight as if nothing more than moderate skill and ordinary care in making the observations would be necessary in order to secure trustworthy results, or, at least, a very close approximation to the truth. The earliest formulæ proposed in this connection, however, were necessarily imperfect. The laws governing the changes of density in the atmosphere as the altitude increases were not known, and it was not possible to determine the actual weight of a given volume of air with a sufficient degree of accuracy.

Laplace * was the first to propose a complete formula which should take account of all the effects of varying temperature and variations in the intensity of the earth's gravitation at different latitudes and at different heights above the surface. The theoretical correctness of Laplace's formula has remained essentially undisputed, and yet there is a wide difference of opinion, even among those best qualified to judge, as to the degree of accuracy actually attainable in barometric measurements of altitude. The prevalent idea among civil engineers is, that the barometer is not a trustworthy instru-

---

* Mécanique Céleste, Tom. IV. pp. 289 - 293. Paris, 1805.

ment in comparison with the spirit-level; and there is undoubtedly considerable ground for this belief. When the heights of important points determined barometrically by different observers, at different seasons of the year, and under different meteorological conditions, are compared with each other, the discrepancies are frequently much too great to be accounted for by any errors of observation. It would seem as if the method or the formula must be at fault.

On the other hand, the impression given by the text-books generally in use in the colleges and scientific schools of the country is, that it is only necessary to multiply observations and take the mean of the results in order to attain to any desired degree of accuracy; and there is no doubt that the publication by the Smithsonian Institution of the well-known tables for the use of meteorological observers, prepared by Professor Guyot, has contributed largely to the very favorable opinion in which the barometer is held in many quarters.

In the introduction to his table arranged for English measures Professor Guyot has given a number of examples, in which the results of the computation of barometric observations are compared with those obtained by means of the spirit-level or from trigonometrical calculations, and the coincidence is in all cases quite remarkable, — amounting, in fact, almost to identity. His words are as follows (Series D, page 34): "The close agreement of the determinations furnished by Laplace's formula, in barometrical measurements carefully conducted, made in favorable circumstances and during the warm season, with those obtained from repeated trigonometrical observations or by the spirit-level, strongly testifies in favor of its general correctness." He then gives several examples of wonderfully close agreement of barometrical with trigonometrical results, and adds: "These figures show conclusively that when the errors which may arise from the great variability of the data furnished by the instruments have been removed by a repetition, in various states of the atmosphere, and by a proper combination of simultaneous observations at stations not too distant from each other, those which remain and may be attributed to the formula cannot be considerable. But, on the other hand, we have no right to expect such results from single observations, taken perhaps in unsettled weather, without paying any regard to the time of the day at which they were made, to the distance or the non-simultaneity of the corresponding observations, or to other unfavorable circumstances." Of the nature of the unfavorable circumstances alluded to, or of the proper time of day, or of the character of the favorable circumstances required to bring about such favorable results, no hint whatever is here given. The most that could be inferred would be that it is necessary to make the measurements "in the warm season," and repeat the observations "in various states of the atmosphere." The remarkably well-agreeing results given, however, were all computed from observations taken on a single day, excepting in one case where the observations extended over parts of two days. The practical result has been that it is almost universally taught, in this country at least, that care and repetition of the observations during a good part of a day will be sufficient to secure satisfactory results. It is true that on pages 80 – 82 of the same series Professor Guyot has given tables of corrections, in French measures, to be applied for different hours of the day to the approximate results obtained in the ordinary way, and thus admitted the existence of important sources of error; but these corrections he neglected to take into account in his own measurements, and thus contributed largely to the belief that they were less important than they really are.

Intermediate between these extremely favorable and extremely unfavorable views belong the opinions of the great majority of geologists and geographers, who, neither requiring nor expecting extreme accuracy, find the barometer an indispensable instrument upon their surveys and reconnoissances, since with its aid they are enabled to secure results sufficiently accurate for their purposes, while without it they would have no results at all, — the determination of differences of altitude with the spirit-level, if the distances are great, being a very laborious and costly operation. A sufficient proof, indeed, if anything additional is needed, that the barometer is a hypsometric instrument of great value, is found in the fact that it has been very widely used in all parts of the world, not only for measuring high mountains, but also for determining the limits of the distribution of plants, the relative position of geological formations, and the most available routes for long lines of railway across rough and thinly settled regions. It was entirely by means of trial lines run with the barometer that the easiest route for the Central Pacific Railroad was found.

The value of the barometer as a field instrument has been seen to great advantage during the progress of the California Survey. It was evident at the outset, owing to the great size of the State, its mountainous character, and the fact that so large a portion was practically unexplored, that the barometer would have to be a chief dependence, and in many cases the sole means available, in procuring the necessary data for the determination of important geological and topographical questions; and, as the work has gone on, it has grown more and more clear that, without its aid, much that has been accomplished would have remained undone, or even unattempted. At the same time it has been well understood that the results obtained in this way were to be regarded only as approximations, varying more or less from the truth, — the amount of variation depending upon certain unknown or imperfectly known conditions.

It was found, for instance, that observations taken in midsummer indicated a greater difference of altitude between two given points than similar observations taken in the spring or fall; that the results obtained from morning or evening observations differed from those obtained from midday observations, the latter being invariably the greater; and that the difference of altitude between two points determined directly was apt to differ from that obtained with aid of one or more intermediate stations; but it was not possible to tell which of these discordant results was the most trustworthy. The discrepancies were obvious; their explanation and correction were matters of great difficulty. Questions concerning the probabilities of error in using the barometer were of constant recurrence; and it was at length determined to enter upon an extended investigation, with the view of ascertaining, if possible, the probable error of any single observation, or of constructing a table of corrections to be applied to the results obtained under different conditions. A detailed account of the method of procedure adopted in this investigation will be given further on; but first it will be necessary to understand clearly the exact conditions of the problem.

The problem is not new. Discrepancies similar to those mentioned above have attracted attention wherever any extended use of the barometer in measuring altitudes has been attempted, and the subject has been repeatedly examined from a great variety of standpoints. During the century and a half which followed the famous experiment of Pascal, in

1648, numerous formulæ were proposed to facilitate the barometric determination of altitudes, in connection with which the names of Mariotte, Halley, Deluc, Playfair, and Schuckburgh were prominent, but which must now be regarded as only having paved the way for the more complete formula of Laplace. The discordant results obtained when this formula, or some modification of it, has been employed are what we have to deal with.

Laplace's original formula comprised four terms, which may be designated as the *pressure* term, including, as is usual, the principal numerical coefficient; the *temperature* term; the correction for *latitude;* and the correction for the change in the height of the mercury column in the barometer caused by the *variation in the intensity of gravity* with increase of altitude. "The corrections depending upon the latitude and upon the variation of gravity are very small; but as they really exist, it is best to notice them, so as to leave in the calculation no other imperfections than those which arise from the inevitable errors of observation; or from the effect of the unknown attractions of the mountains; or from the hygrometrical state of the air, which ought to be noticed; or, finally, from the error arising from the use of the hypothesis relative to the law of the diminution of heat." * This quotation will be sufficient to show what Laplace considered as the possible imperfections of his formula, and to give us a hint as to the probable character of the modifications which would be introduced by subsequent investigators. So far as the corrections for latitude and for variation of gravity are concerned, little need be said. Their numerical values would have to be changed, it is true, whenever improved methods of research should make possible more accurate determinations of the values of the physical constants involved. But, as the only constants to be considered in this connection are the length of a seconds pendulum and the mean radius of the earth, it is evident that the changes, when made, could have only a very small effect upon the final result, — the values of these constants already adopted leaving but little to be desired in the way of accuracy. The addition by Oltmanns of a fifth term, to introduce a small correction depending upon the height of the lower barometer above the sea-level, requires also only a passing mention.

* Mécanique Céleste, Bowditch's translation, Vol. IV. p. 571.

The pressure term and the temperature term, therefore, are the only ones remaining, subject to any essential modification; and in what follows it will be seen how varied in character the modifications proposed have been.

It is necessary to observe, however, that many of the changes which the formula has undergone, though of great importance in themselves, were really less radical than would appear at first sight. As first published the formula was ill-adapted for purposes of calculation. The operations required were complex, and the work was tedious. Transformations were therefore made with the view of reducing the amount of numerical computation, or of securing a tolerable approximation with very little labor, or of adapting the formula to different standards of measure, but not necessarily connected with the idea of remedying any of its deficiencies or increasing its theoretical or practical accuracy. Hypsometrical tables of greater or less extent, some requiring and some avoiding the use of logarithms, and giving results in English, French, or other units of measure, have been published from time to time, but in almost all cases the criterion, according to which the ultimate value of the table was to be judged, was the more or less close agreement of the results with those which would have been obtained if the formula of Laplace had been applied rigorously. The special formula upon which each set of tables was based might differ widely in form, though not in substance, from that of Laplace. The tables proposed by Dr. Benzenberg,* by aid of which an observer performing a few simple additions could tell his altitude at once, form no exception to this statement, for they were calculated upon the theory that it is possible, by the application of Mariotte's law, to determine how thick a layer of the atmosphere must be, at different altitudes, to just balance a column of mercury a hundredth of an inch in height.

The numerical coefficient in the barometric formula can be obtained in two ways. The empirical method consists in comparing the heights determined by exact trigonometrical operations with those obtained from observations of the barometer. In these comparisons this coefficient is regarded as an unknown quantity, and made to satisfy the condition that the two measurements shall be equal. In the second method, which is

---

* See Gilbert's Annalen der Physik, Band XXXVI. 1810. pp. 150–167.

more direct, the coefficient is deduced from a comparison of the specific gravities of air and mercury, but it is evidently subject to any inaccuracies with which these quantities are affected, and can take no account of possible differences in the constitution of the upper atmosphere, which might affect the ratio existing between the weights of equal volumes of these substances at high elevations. The coefficient derived from theoretical considerations alone giving results which were too small, Laplace adopted the empirical value determined by Ramond from measurements made in the Pyrenees. The mountain selected for these measurements was the Pic du Midi de Bigorre, a peak which rises to an altitude of over nine thousand feet above the level of the sea, and which was extremely well situated for experiments of this kind, being comparatively isolated, and not being separated by any intervening ridge from the station on the plain, eight thousand feet below, where the corresponding observations were taken.* The observations were taken in the latter part of September, 1803, and, in all instances, near the middle of the day. It is evident that a coefficient thus determined would be rigorously exact only for measurements under similar conditions. If a mountain in a different latitude had been chosen, or if a different month or a different hour of the day had been selected, or if the measurements had been made upon stormy instead of upon pleasant days, the numerical value of the coefficient would doubtless have been different; how much different it is needless now to inquire. It is sufficient to know that the number finally adopted by Laplace, and published in the "Mécanique Céleste," was the one which seemed most accurate, on the supposition that the lower barometer was at the level of the sea, in latitude 45°, and that the temperature of the air was that of melting ice. What effect the climatic conditions prevailing in the region of the Pyrenees would have upon this coefficient it is not possible to say, but it would not be strange if the coefficient had to be increased or diminished in order to attain the best results in regions where the climate differed much from that of the Pyrenees. This view was, indeed, advanced and defended by the German astronomer, Lindenau,† who, in the construction of his tables, which were

---

* Ramond's Mémoires sur la Formule Barométrique. Paris, 1811. p. 5.
† Lindenau's Tables Barométriques. Gotha, 1809. p. xxxvii.

intended more especially for use in Germany, adopted a value differing to some extent from that fixed by Ramond. The elaborate investigations of Regnault, in the course of which the specific gravities of air and mercury were ascertained to a greater degree of accuracy than ever before, led also to some modifications of the barometric coefficient; a new value, somewhat larger than Ramond's, being adopted by Plantamour[*] in his tables, which, adapted to English measures, have been published by Colonel Williamson in the appendix to his treatise "On the Use of the Barometer."[†]

The changes, however, in the numerical coefficient have been neither great in amount nor of such a nature as to cause the discordant results which have been referred to above to disappear; and it is evident that the cause of the difficulty must be sought elsewhere than in the erroneous estimations of this quantity. It is not unlikely that the coefficient which would give the best results in Europe or in the eastern part of the United States would not be the one best adapted for the climate of California; but it is equally improbable that any important advantage would be gained by any attempt to determine a special coefficient for use on the Pacific coast. The results of Colonel Williamson's examination[‡] into the possibility of assigning values to the barometric constants which shall give a "correct value to the mean difference of altitude, and at the same time make the computed results the same for all the months," can well be taken as conclusive in this respect. The substitution of a coefficient based upon the best modern determinations of specific gravity in the place of the less accurate number adopted by Laplace is an advantage, but does not bring the results obtained under diverse atmospheric conditions into any better accord with each other.

The other portion of the pressure term of Laplace's formula depends upon the supposition that the atmosphere is in a condition of equilibrium, and that the column of mercury in the barometer is balanced by a column of air reaching to the outer limit of the atmosphere. Were all the forces which tend to cause motion in the atmosphere to cease acting,

---

[*] Mémoires de la Société de Physique et d'Histoire Naturelle de Genève. Tom. XIII. 1852. pp. 53 note, and 66.

[†] Professional Papers of the Corps of Engineers, U. S. Army, No. 15. 1867.

[‡] Pages 221 – 228 of the work just cited.

this supposed condition of equilibrium would soon be attained; but so long as these forces act there must always be a greater or less inaccuracy in the supposition, and a corresponding error in the results obtained from using the formula. This source of error cannot be avoided entirely, — at least not from any theoretical considerations; and the only resource left us is to reject or to assign less weight to observations taken at times of manifestly unusual atmospheric disturbance. From two other points of view, however, this term has been supposed to be faulty. Dr. Benzenberg,[*] applying Dalton's law relating to mixtures of independent gases, was convinced that each of the four principal components of the atmosphere — namely, oxygen, nitrogen, carbonic acid, and aqueous vapor — acted upon the barometric column independently of the others, and that each followed a special law of diminution in density with increase of altitude; so that, to secure perfect results, four pressure terms were really necessary. The density of the oxygen atmosphere would decrease more rapidly than that of the nitrogen, and that of the carbonic acid more rapidly than either; and the volumes of these gases in the atmosphere would thus be proportionally different at different altitudes. Instead of changing the formula Benzenberg prepared a table of corrections to be applied to the calculated results; from which it appears that the correction is negative for altitudes less than about thirty-four thousand feet (the maximum numerical value being 30.9 feet for altitudes of fifteen thousand feet), and positive for higher elevations. At first sight it seems as if these corrections must be made, but experiment has shown that air collected at all elevations above the surface, in balloon ascents, contains oxygen and nitrogen in almost precisely the same proportions. Owing to the extreme mobility and continued agitation of the air, the state of equilibrium in which the gases would be arranged as Benzenberg supposed is never attained, and consequently the necessity for the corrections vanishes.[†] Bessel's discussion,[‡] moreover, of the distribution of aqueous vapor in the

[*] Gilbert's Annalen der Physik, Band XLII. 1812. pp. 162–176.

[†] In "Air and Rain," London, 1872, Dr. Robert Angus Smith cites a considerable number of analyses in which there seems to be evidence of a slightly smaller percentage of oxygen at high altitudes; but as this is explained by an accompanying change in the amount of carbonic acid present, it cannot be regarded as justifying Benzenberg's corrections. Compare, also, Herschel's Meteorology, p. 21.

[‡] Astronomische Nachrichten, No. 357 ; Altona, 1838.

atmosphere seems to be decisive against the theory, in its fulness, that each gas or vapor in the air, or other mixture of gases, is exposed only to the pressure of its own particles.

The second criticism referred to is, that Laplace erred in considering the effective air column as a vertical cylinder rather than as a portion of a cone whose vertex is at the centre of the earth. Dr. Ohm * has the credit of first calling attention to this point. His formula is simpler in some respects than that of Laplace, and was received with considerable favor, though practically, as observed by Professor Rogg,† the simplification amounts to no more than doing away with the correction for the variation in the intensity of gravity. The same observation was also made by Zech,‡ in his approving notice of Ohm's formula. On the other hand, Professor Guldberg § of Christiania has well shown that it was Ohm, after all, instead of Laplace, who was in fault by neglecting, in the development of his formula, the effects of lateral pressures.

The conclusion is therefore inevitable that the pressure term, at least, is to be considered essentially unalterable, — no change having been proposed which can be regarded as an improvement or as likely to be of service in diminishing the discrepancies whose removal is desired.

There remains, then, the *temperature term* to be examined. With every increase of temperature the air column expands, or, what amounts to the same thing, a relatively larger portion of the mass of the air is found above the higher of two barometers; and the difference of altitude between them, as estimated from the barometric readings, will be less than it would have been if the air had remained constantly at the lower temperature. Any increase of moisture in the atmosphere would evidently have a similar effect, — aqueous vapor being specifically lighter than air. Both these effects are provided for by the temperature term, as commonly written, which consequently becomes subject to change from two points of view.

The value of the correction for temperature, independently of moisture, depends upon the absolute rate of expansion of air by heat and upon

* Ohm's Grundzüge der Physik, Nuremberg, 1853. pp. 182–193.
† See Schlömilch's Zeitschrift für Mathematik und Physik, Band 7. 1862. p. 144.
‡ Astronomische Nachrichten, Band XLI. 1855. p. 40.
§ See Schlömilch's Zeitschrift, Band 7, pp. 359–363.

the law which governs the decrease of temperature as the altitude increases. The coefficient of expansion of air has been determined with such nicety that no further change need be expected in that direction; but the case is otherwise with the law of decrease of temperature. This law, in fact, is not known; and it seems scarcely probable that any law will ever be discovered which will explain all the observed facts. Were the atmosphere subject to fewer changes and disturbances, the chances for detecting such a law would be greater, and there would be more encouragement for undertaking an investigation with that object in view. As the case stands, the only course left is to adopt some hypothesis which shall either simplify the formula or shall be most in harmony with well-grounded theoretical considerations. The hypothesis adopted by Laplace, avowedly for the sake of simplicity, and justified by the consideration that only "a small interval in comparison with the whole height of the atmosphere" is in question, was that the temperature decreases "nearly in an arithmetical progression" from one station to the other;[*] which is nearly the same as supposing the temperature of the air column to be uniform throughout, and equal to the mean of the temperatures at the lower and upper stations. This hypothesis also assumes that two columns of air, exposed to the same pressure, have the same height, whether the temperature decreases or increases from below upwards, provided only the mean temperature remains unaffected.

Here seems to be a weak point in the formula; for, had any other hypothesis been adopted, a different value for the temperature correction would have been obtained. Lindenau[†] was one of the first to suggest a change. Comparing the results of his study of the laws of astronomical refraction with direct thermometric observations at different altitudes, he was led to the conclusion that the temperature decreases less rapidly in the upper than in the lower regions of the atmosphere; and, following in the track of Euler and of Oriani, he assumed that the decrease of temperature was in accordance with an harmonic progression,[‡] and constructed

---

[*] Mécanique Céleste, Bowditch's Translation, Vol. IV. p. 566.

[†] Tables Barométriques, p. xxxviii.

[‡] Three numbers, arranged in decreasing order of size, form an *harmonic proportion* when the difference of the first and the second is to the difference of the second and the third as the first is to the third. In a series of numbers arranged as an *harmonic progression*, any three consecutive terms form an *harmonic proportion*.

his tables on this basis. This hypothesis, however, instead of simplify-
ing, complicates the formula, and contributes little or nothing to its accuracy; for the law of decrease of temperature is still left in doubt. In
other respects the researches of Lindenau belong among the most important contributions to the subject of barometric hypsometry, and his his-
torical sketch of the development of the earlier formulæ was much more
complete than anything that had preceded.

A more important alteration in the form of the temperature correction
has been proposed by General Baeyer.* On the ground that the atmosphere, or at least that portion of it with which barometric calculations
would have to deal, derives its heat principally from the earth, and only
to a comparatively small degree from the direct rays of the sun, he assumed that the rate of decrease of temperature in the successive strata
of the atmosphere would vary as the square of their distances from the
centre of the earth; and he represented the difference of temperature between the upper and lower stations by a series of terms in which the
first and second powers of these distances, together with constant coefficients whose values were to be determined empirically, were involved.
The determination of the numerical values of these coefficients was to be
based upon the effects of refraction, for in this way the actual variations
in the density of the air column would be taken into account, and the
influence of possible local disturbances of temperature at the extreme
stations be avoided. General Baeyer's mathematical treatment of the
problem is elaborate, but not in all particulars satisfactory. For altitudes of less than six thousand feet, he assumes, for reasons which are
not clearly stated, that certain terms in his series may be neglected;
and he finally adopts an expression which makes the difference of temperature between two stations increase directly as their difference of
altitude, thus apparently abandoning the special hypothesis which was
to make his formula essentially different from that of Laplace. The
examination of the conditions of the problem for greater altitudes he
seems not to have entered upon. The principal temperature coefficient,
moreover, whose value was deduced from observations upon atmospheric
refraction, was found not to be strictly a constant. This is readily ex-

---

* Astronomische Nachrichten, Band XLI. 1855, pp. 305–336 ; and Poggendorff's Annalen
der Physik und Chemie, Band XCVIII. 1856, pp. 371–396.

plained, if we admit, as we must, that the actual rate of decrease of temperature with increase of altitude does not in all cases and under all circumstances follow the same law. A mean value for this coefficient is employed in the formula in order to obtain a first approximate difference of altitude, which, in its turn, is used to get a special value of the coefficient, which will correspond better with the actual conditions of the case in hand. The results obtained in this way differ in a slight degree from those given by Laplace's formula; but, as will appear further on, they are not free from the irregularities and imperfections previously referred to, which it is so desirable to explain or correct. The conclusion reached, after a careful study of General Baeyer's discussion, is that, even if we are willing to allow that his hypothesis rests on a firmer theoretical basis than that of Laplace, the slight advantages gained, doubtful at best, are more than counterbalanced by the complexity of the formula and the character of the numerical operations required in its use.

The two principal, and possibly the only radical changes proposed in the correction for temperature alone thus appear to have yielded no valuable results; and the simpler hypothesis of Laplace may well be accepted as practically the best in the present state of our knowledge of the physics of the atmosphere.

In Laplace's formula the correction for the effect of moisture is introduced by increasing the value of the temperature correction by about one tenth of its whole amount; an increase which in many cases will correspond very well to the actual hygrometric condition of the atmosphere, and which has the additional advantage of shortening to some extent the numerical computations. But no claim for accuracy can be urged in its favor. In fact, when the mean temperature of the air column between two barometric stations falls below the freezing-point of water, this mode of accounting for the effects of moisture actually introduces an error; for the temperature term in this case is subtractive, while the correction for moisture should still be additive.*

Bessel, in his " Bemerkungen über barometrisches Höhenmessen," † seems

---

* Compare a paper by Dr. Apjohn, in the Proceedings of the Royal Irish Academy, Vol. II. 1844. p. 564. This is the earliest mention of this source of error which I have met with.

† Astronomische Nachrichten, Nos. 356, 357; Altona, 1838.

to have been the first to give the question of a separate correction for the effect of moisture a thorough investigation. His discussion of the subject is quite long, and the resulting formula considerably more complex than that of Laplace, though not difficult to adapt for computation with the aid of appropriate tables. In the employment of this formula it is necessary to know the fraction which represents the humidity of the air-column between the two stations, for which in practice, in the absence of better data, the mean of the humidities at the extreme stations may be substituted.

Formulæ introducing a special vapor correction have also been published by Plantamour, Williamson, Bauernfeind, Renny, Rühlmann, and others. Plantamour's formula * differs from that of Bessel principally in the augmented value of the numerical coefficient, and was the one chosen by Colonel Williamson for translation into English measures. The investigations of Dr. Bauernfeind † were going on nearly at the same time as those of Plantamour, and led to nearly the same results, so far as the improvement of the barometric formula is concerned. Of the other interesting and valuable meteorological results of his investigations it is not necessary here to speak. Renny, ‡ who appears also to have been an original investigator in this field, applied the vapor correction by subtracting from the observed heights of the mercury column the amounts due to the tension of the aqueous vapor, avoiding in this way any reference to the relative humidity. The results obtained, however, by the use of this formula are practically identical with those derived from Plantamour's. Neither does Rühlmann's formula § differ essentially from the two just mentioned, but it contains, more for the sake of completeness than from any hope of additional practical benefit, a small term intended to take into account the effect of the attractions of the mountain masses themselves.

Theoretically the formulæ of this type must be regarded as the most

---

* Mémoires de la Société de Physique et d'Histoire naturelle de Genève, Tom. XIII. 1852. p. 63.

† Beobachtungen und Untersuchungen über die Genauigkeit barometrischer Höhenmessungen, etc. München, 1862.

‡ Transactions of the Royal Irish Academy, Vol. XXIII. 1859. pp. 437 – 448, and 623 – 668.

§ Die barometrischen Höhenmessungen, etc. Leipzig, 1870.

nearly perfect, and under favorable circumstances they will doubtless give results which are a closer approximation to the truth, and more in accord with each other than those obtained when the temperature and moisture corrections are combined in one. For, during the warm season, when the air is relatively dry, the combination of the two corrections in one increases a quantity which is already too large, while for the winter, or wet season, the moisture correction is underestimated, and a quantity already too small is still further diminished. The principal difficulty in the way of a more general adoption of this type of formula lies in the uncertainty attending the observations which have to be depended upon in estimating the humidity of the air. When the mean of a long series can be used, it is possible to approximate quite closely to the real mean humidity, but the error of any single observation may well be fully equal to that introduced by combining into one both the temperature and moisture corrections. In general, Laplace's formula will give higher results than Plantamour's in countries where the climate is dry, and lower where the climate is moist. The numerical values of these differences in two cases are shown in the following table, which is made up from Tables LIII. and LIV. of Williamson : —

TABLE SHOWING THE EFFECT OF A SEPARATE CORRECTION FOR MOISTURE.

	Jan.	Feb.	Mar.	Apr.	May.	June.	July	Aug.	Sept.	Oct.	Nov.	Dec.	Mean.	Range.
I.	21.5	19.1	15.7	11.3	7.4	7.3	5.7	7.0	8.6	11.6	15.8	19.8	12.6	15.8
II.	4.4	3.0	1.3	−2.5	−4.0	−6.0	−7.7	−3.2	−6.0	−2.1	0.7	4.2	−1.5	12.1

Case I. is that of Geneva and St. Bernard in Switzerland, whose difference of altitude is 6791.4 feet. The separate calculation of the vapor correction gives for every month of the year a higher value than is obtained when it is combined with the temperature correction, showing that for this particular case Laplace's arbitrary increase of the temperature term was insufficient. Case II. is that of Sacramento and Fort Churchill, where the difference of altitude amounts to about 4,238 feet. From April to October the atmosphere is very dry, and the true correction for moisture is seen to be less than that involved in Laplace's formula, though the two results from yearly means agree remarkably well.

The range of the differences amounts, in the first case, to 15.8 feet; which is sufficient to remove only about one-fifth part of the discrepancy between the results obtained in summer and in winter, as will be seen from the following table, which gives the computed difference of altitude between Geneva and St. Bernard for each month of the year, from the mean of observations continued through six years, and their variations from the true difference determined by spirit-level. The grand mean for the six years is 6782.4 feet, which is less than the true altitude by nine feet.

COMPUTED DIFFERENCE OF ALTITUDE BETWEEN GENEVA AND ST. BERNARD.

By Spirit-Level 6791.4 feet.					
January	6745.5	− 45.9	July	6820.9	+ 29.5
February	6762.5	− 28.9	August	6807.8	+ 16.4
March	6788.8	− 2.6	September	6784.8	− 6.6
April	6794.3	+ 2.9	October	6757.9	− 33.5
May	6799.3	+ 7.9	November	6759.6	− 31.8
June	6819.3	+ 27.9	December......	6747.8	− 43.6

The range of error amounts here to 75.4 feet, although the computations were made with the aid of tables which introduce the special moisture correction, and the conditions were favorable for obtaining the best agreeing results.

The different portions of the formula have now been made to pass in review, and it appears that no changes in its form or in the numerical values of its constant terms have been sufficient to overcome entirely the observed discrepancies. The further discussion of the problem will be the subject of the next chapter.

CHAPTER II.

DETAILED ACCOUNT OF THE INVESTIGATION IN CALIFORNIA.

FROM the summary account given in Chapter I. of the principal changes which have been proposed since the time of Laplace for the sake of increasing the accuracy of barometric measurements, it will be evident that, after all the real improvements have been incorporated into the formula, there is still a source of uncertainty in the results obtained, which requires a further examination. It was an investigation of this kind which was entered upon by the California Survey, the primary object being to secure a table of corrections which could be used for increasing or diminishing the heights computed from observations taken under widely varying conditions, at different seasons of the year and at all hours of the day, so as to attain as close an approximation to the truth as possible. The same table would also serve to indicate the hour of the day in each month of the year at which the nearest approach to truth would be attained.

At the time the investigation was begun it was not known to any one connected with the Survey that any similar tables had ever been published, or that the subject had been approached from this direction; and even if the many curious and instructive results which a rather extensive examination of the literature of hypsometry since the beginning of the present century has brought to light had been known, the necessity for undertaking the California investigation would have been in no wise diminished, the climatic conditions on the slopes of the Sierra Nevada differing in so many respects from those of Europe or Asia. The brief sketch of the labors of others upon this subject which will be given in Chapter III. will show, moreover, that no practical benefit appears to have been derived from the tables published or the suggestions made. There is no reason to believe that systematic corrections, to eliminate the errors due to the season of the year at which the observations were taken, have ever been applied to any extensive series of barometric measurement either in this country or in Europe.

With the single exception of Colonel Williamson's work, to which reference has already been made, there has been nothing of importance published, which has any direct bearing upon the special phases of the problem, as it presents itself upon the Pacific coast of the United States. Had he been able to continue his investigations, he would doubtless have given this portion of the subject the same careful study, and published the results with the same painstaking thoroughness, which marks his previous labors. In a certain sense the present investigation may be regarded as supplementary to his, but its claims to originality and novelty are beyond question.

The first requisite in the investigation was the accumulation of trustworthy observations, taken at stated times and continued regularly for a long period, at points whose differences of altitude were known from careful surveys with the spirit-level. A year's observations, at least, would be necessary to furnish data for estimating the effects of the changes in the atmosphere with the change of seasons; and a much longer series, to eliminate the possible abnormal conditions prevailing during any one month. The results of the first year's observations were, on the whole, satisfactory, and fully justified the continuance of the investigation for a longer period. The second year's results agreed in the main quite well with those of the first year, although there were unexpectedly large variations in certain months, and it was decided to prepare a first set of tables at the end of the third year, which would be available for immediate use and until they were superseded by more accurate tables, based upon additional observations. The investigation had to be suspended, however, after the third year, from lack of funds, and the additional observations have not been taken. The instruments used were all made by James Green of New York, and consisted of cistern barometers, with verniers reading to two thousandths of an inch, and standard thermometers, so graduated that it was possible to estimate tenths of a Fahrenheit degree with ease. There was at each station a pair of these thermometers, the bulb of one being kept wet while the other was dry, thus furnishing the data for estimating the amount of moisture in the air. They were protected from the effects of reflected heat as well as from the direct rays of the sun, and placed in all cases several feet above the ground, in such positions that there would always be a free circulation of air about them. The barometers were compared with each other and with the standard barometer at the Survey office, both at the beginning of the work and subsequently whenever a visit to the stations made such comparisons possible. A record of the index errors was kept and the proper corrections applied to all the readings preliminary to the computations.

The points selected as observing stations were Sacramento, Colfax, and Summit, on the line of the Central Pacific Railroad, the altitude of each station being known from the railroad surveys. Every possible assistance was given by the officers of the railroad, and at Colfax and Summit the instruments were set up in buildings belonging to the company. At Sacramento the observations were taken on L Street, at the house of Mr. A. A. Freeman, an employee of the railroad company as draughtsman in the office of the chief engineer. At Sacramento and Colfax the position of the instruments remained unchanged during the whole three years, but at Summit one change was made necessary before the expiration of the first half-year by the removal of the company's office to a more convenient spot near the hotel. The barometer hung about four feet higher in its new position, for which allowance was made in the computations.

The observations at Sacramento were taken by Mr. Freeman, or some substitute during any temporary absence, and furnish a nearly unbroken record of the changes of pressure, temperature, and moisture in the atmosphere for the three years. The observer at Colfax was the station-agent, Mr. J. P. Hodgdon, or his assistant, Mr. Logner. The monthly returns from Colfax were not quite so complete as those from Sacramento, and at one time the barometer was out of order so that no observations could be taken for five days. The accidental omissions, which averaged two a month, were so scattered that it was generally possible to interpolate a suitable value within such narrow limits of error that the value of the monthly means would not be perceptibly affected.

At Summit the number of sporadic omissions was smaller than at Colfax, but breaks of a longer duration were, unfortunately, more frequent. At one time there was an interruption of ten days, caused by the breaking of the barometer; and at other times there were intervals of thirteen days and of five days in which no readings of the barometer were taken. The observations at Summit also came to an end a month before the close of the third year by the death of the observer, news of which was not received by the director of the Survey in time to make arrangements for the continuance of the work by his successor at the office. Several accidents, moreover, happened to the thermometers. During the first winter they were both broken, and they could not be replaced from New York for four months. For this interval there were no observations with the wet bulb, and the place of the dry bulb was supplied by a thermometer belonging to the railroad company. This thermometer was found to give results agreeing very closely with those of Green's standard thermometers, and it was not thought necessary to apply any correction to its readings. During the second winter the wet-bulb thermometer was reported "broken by the snow," and there was a consequent interruption in the psychrometric observations until a new thermometer could be sent from San Francisco. The record of the observations of the psychrometer shows, furthermore, that good results cannot be obtained during the cold weather without extraordinary care on the part of the observer. At Summit the wet-bulb thermometer, for a large part of each winter season, was recorded as standing within one or two degrees of the freezing-point of water, though the temperature of the air might be as much as twenty or thirty degrees lower. The only explanation of this is that the observers did not watch for the effects of the evaporation of the film of ice which formed about the bulb of the thermometer, but recorded the reading too soon after moistening the bulb.

Another cause of the irregularity at Summit was the frequent change of observer, which occurred whenever a change was made by the railroad company in the agent in charge of the station. Mr. C. F. Gooding had charge of the instruments at this point for the first four months, and was followed by Messrs. Wales, Potter, Stewart, Shearer, and Haskins in succession, all of whom had to be instructed in the methods of observing. Their short terms of service naturally interfered with their becoming skilled observers. Nevertheless, the work seems to have been done for the most part conscientiously, and the inevitable errors of observation may fairly be considered as eliminated from the monthly means, excepting so far as relates to the wet bulb for the times when the temperature was below thirty-two degrees. The Summit record for the month of August, 1873, however, presented so many anomalies that it was impossible to avoid the conclusion that the observations were imperfect or that errors had crept into the record in copying. For this reason the results of this month's work have been considered of less value and allowed less weight in the final discussions.

The distances of the stations from each other in a straight line and their differences of altitude according to the railroad surveys are as follows : —

	Distance.	Difference of altitude.
Sacramento to Colfax	45 miles	2,399 feet
Colfax to Summit	36 "	4,590 "
Sacramento to Summit	77 "	6,989 "

The absolute altitudes of the railroad stations at these points are given as 31, 2,425, and 7,017 feet respectively, but the difference of altitudes given above takes into account the actual position of the barometers, above or below the level of the railroad track. The approximate latitude of Sacramento is 38° 35', of Colfax 39° 7', and of Summit 39° 20'.

Sacramento, though so nearly at the level of the sea, is shut off by the coast ranges of mountains, except through a narrow opening by which the river makes its way to the ocean, from the sea-breezes which are so strong at San Francisco, and other direct effects of the vicinity of large bodies of water. As a meteorological station it is an excellent representative of the great valley of California, which stretches from the southeast to the northwest between the coast ranges and the Sierra Nevada, and which, from the nature of things, must be the base of operations in almost all the surveys of the mountains on either side. In all barometric work in the Sierra or on the eastern slope of the coast ranges much better results will be obtained if the station barometer is kept in the neighborhood of Sacramento, than would be the case if San Francisco, or other point directly on the coast, were used as a base, though the absolute altitude of the two points above the sea-level might be the same. The results of an attempt to determine barometrically the difference of level between San Francisco and Sacramento, given on page 48, will illustrate in a very marked manner the effect of the differences of climate on the two sides of the coast ranges.

The town of Colfax lies on the ridge between the valley of Bear River and that of the North Fork of the American, which is followed by the railroad in its ascent of the mountains. It is not shut in by hills on either side, nor so exposed as to be swept by violent winds or affected by other local causes of atmospheric disturbance. Snow falls only at rare intervals, and never lies upon the ground for any length of time. Although over 2,400 feet above the sea-level, the mean temperature of Colfax from June to January is actually higher than that of Sacramento, which proves the station to have been well chosen as a means of getting data for the study of the peculiar effects of the abnormally warm belt of country which stretches along the foot-hills parallel to the general trend of the valley.

At Summit the conditions are not quite so favorable. The railroad station stands a short distance below the culminating point of Donner Pass, near the west end of the tunnel, a third of a mile in length, by means of which the crossing of the ridge is effected. The enclosing hills on either side rise with considerable steepness for several hundred feet, though not so abruptly as to produce the effect of a gorge. The prevailing winds are deflected somewhat by the ridges which bound the approaches to the pass, and this may possibly have some influence upon the temperature; how much it is impossible to say. A more serious obstacle in the way of getting perfectly satisfactory observations for temperature is presented by the sheds built over the railroad track to keep it clear from snow, which accumulates during the winter to the depth of twenty feet or more at this part of the mountains. The snow-sheds are extended so as to include the railroad office and the approach to the hotel during the worst of the winter, and thus the thermometers may not have been fairly exposed to the open air all the time the observations were going on. In making the necessary reductions and computations, these sources of error were kept in mind, and any unusual or remarkable deviations examined with care.

The observations were taken three times a day, — at 7 A. M., 2 P. M., and 9 P. M., the hours recommended for the observers who collect meteorological data for the Smithsonian Institution. From observations taken at these three hours, it has been found that a very good daily mean can be obtained by taking simply the mean of the observations, and it was not thought necessary to adopt any more accurate method of ascertaining this mean; such, for instance, as those recommended by Colonel Williamson.* Hourly observations, if they could have been obtained, would have given results worthy of a higher degree of confidence, it is true, but, with the limited means available for the prosecution of this work, it is doubtful if the extra degree of refinement attained would have justified the outlay of money and time requisite for the numerical reductions and computations. The observations were sent at the close of each month to the office of the Survey at San Francisco, and the reductions were made as rapidly as the nature of the case would permit. The barometric readings were first corrected for temperature, and then increased or diminished by the amount of the index error, so as to bring all the data into harmony with the same unchanging standard. No index error was applied to the readings of the thermometers. The following tables show the mean height of the barometer and the mean temperature for the different months and hours of the day for the whole time the observations were continued. The work was begun at Summit and Colfax earlier than at Sacramento, so that the means of September, 1870, are inserted for those two stations, though the computed results for September, 1870, have not been used in the subsequent course of the investigation. The means of the wet-bulb thermometer have not been included, partly because of the incompleteness of the record, and partly because use was not made of them in the computations. In some cases the means given were derived from observations extending over only a part of a month, but in only one month were observations lacking for more than eight days. For July, 1872, the means for Summit are derived from observations continued only from the first to the fifteenth of the month. The completeness of the record at Sacramento usually served as a guide in estimating how far the results derived from incomplete data could be regarded as fair representatives of the monthly record, and did away with the necessity of giving any further special discussion to those cases.

* On the Use of the Barometer, p. 158.

MONTHLY MEANS OF BAROMETER AND THERMOMETER
AT SACRAMENTO. (BAROMETER REDUCED TO 32° F.)

Month and Hour.	BAROMETER.				THERMOMETER.			
	1870.	1871.	1872.	1873.	1870.	1871.	1872.	1873.
January 7 A.M.	....	30.173	30.158	30.152	......	38.1	42.0	44.8
2 P.M.	....	30.141	30.157	30.131	......	52.8	49.2	57.6
9 P.M.	....	30.148	30.166	30.135	......	44.7	45.4	49.7
MEAN	....	30.154	30.160	30.139	......	45.2	45.5	50.7
February 7 A.M.	....	30.103	30.087	30.076	......	39.4	47.6	41.9
2 P.M.	....	30.088	30.071	30.054	......	54.1	55.5	54.6
9 P.M.	....	30.083	30.082	30.065	......	47.3	50.8	47.8
MEAN	....	30.091	30.080	30.065	......	46.9	51.3	48.1
March 7 A.M.	....	30.146	30.111	30.143	......	45.5	48.0	48.9
2 P.M.	....	30.140	30.074	30.118	......	62.4	60.3	65.8
9 P.M.	....	30.114	30.080	30.125	......	54.6	53.2	54.8
MEAN	....	30.133	30.088	30.129	......	54.2	53.8	56.5
April 7 A.M.	....	30.016	30.079	30.106	......	49.3	51.8	58.6
2 P.M.	....	29.997	30.038	30.085	......	67.3	64.6	70.3
9 P.M.	....	29.976	30.049	30.113	......	56.8	56.6	57.9
MEAN	....	29.996	30.055	30.101	......	57.8	57.7	62.3
May 7 A.M.	....	29.992	29.954	29.920	......	53.6	62.4	63.3
2 P.M.	....	29.965	29.910	29.901	......	71.2	76.2	76.5
9 P.M.	....	29.962	29.917	29.898	......	59.5	62.4	64.5
MEAN	....	29.973	29.927	29.906	......	61.4	67.0	68.1
June 7 A.M.	....	29.939	29.943	29.971	......	61.9	64.5	67.7
2 P.M.	....	29.914	29.897	29.961	......	84.1	78.0	80.7
9 P.M.	....	29.896	29.914	29.957	......	68.6	65.2	67.4
MEAN	....	29.916	29.918	29.963	......	71.5	69.2	71.9
July 7 A.M.	....	29.914	29.930	29.909	......	60.3	66.0	70.2
2 P.M.	....	29.883	29.882	29.871	......	85.0	82.2	86.7
9 P.M.	....	29.869	29.880	29.894	......	68.3	68.2	76.4
MEAN	....	29.889	29.897	29.891	......	71.2	72.1	77.8
August 7 A.M.	....	29.918	29.911	29.987	......	60.8	63.5	63.0
2 P.M.	....	29.878	29.864	29.943	......	89.6	82.0	81.6
9 P.M.	....	29.861	29.863	29.967	......	69.8	67.6	63.6
MEAN	....	29.886	29.879	29.966	......	73.4	71.0	69.4
September 7 A.M.	....	29.932	29.944	29.932	......	55.2	59.4	60.1
2 P.M.	....	29.897	29.905	29.874	......	79.9	77.7	81.9
9 P.M.	....	29.885	29.916	29.915	......	65.2	64.5	62.8
MEAN	....	29.905	29.921	29.907	......	66.8	67.2	68.3
October 7 A.M.	29.980	30.032	30.022	....	49.3	49.7	51.5	......
2 P.M.	29.949	29.989	29.973	....	72.6	74.0	72.2	......
9 P.M.	29.949	29.984	29.984	....	57.3	58.6	56.9	......
MEAN	29.959	30.001	29.993	....	59.8	60.8	60.0	......
November 7 A.M.	30.131	30.068	30.165	....	42.0	42.0	43.6	......
2 P.M.	30.093	30.043	30.110	....	62.9	60.1	60.8	......
9 P.M.	30.106	30.046	30.133	....	50.1	47.5	47.8	......
MEAN	30.110	30.052	30.136	....	51.7	49.9	50.7	......
December 7 A.M.	30.179	30.116	30.071	....	34.7	42.9	42.2	......
2 P.M.	30.142	30.090	30.056	....	50.6	50.3	54.5	......
9 P.M.	30.152	30.101	30.070	....	41.9	45.7	45.6	......
MEAN	30.158	30.102	30.066	....	42.4	46.3	47.4	......
MEAN OF 7 A.M.	....	30.029	30.031	....	......	49.9	53.5	......
YEAR 2 P.M.	....	30.002	29.995	....	......	69.2	67.8	......
9 P.M.	....	29.994	30.004	....	......	57.2	57.0	......
GRAND MEAN	....	30.008	30.010	....	......	58.8	59.4	......

MONTHLY MEANS OF BAROMETER AND THERMOMETER
AT COLFAX. (BAROMETER REDUCED TO 32° F.)

Month and Hour.		BAROMETER.				THERMOMETER.			
		1870.	1871.	1872.	1873.	1870.	1871.	1872.	1873.
January	7 A.M.	....	27.632	27.608	27.634	......	40.9	40.4	45.9
	2 P.M.	....	27.607	27.607	27.595	......	55.9	53.8	57.9
	9 P.M.	....	27.627	27.616	27.629	......	44.9	43.9	49.2
	MEAN	....	27.622	27.610	27.619	......	47.2	46.1	51.0
February	7 A.M.	....	27.543	27.555	27.510	......	37.6	43.9	37.0
	2 P.M.	....	27.540	27.547	27.505	......	50.2	53.2	47.4
	9 P.M.	....	27.524	27.563	27.516	......	42.3	47.3	39.9
	MEAN	....	27.536	27.555	27.510	......	43.4	48.1	41.4
March	7 A.M.	....	27.599	27.564	27.614	......	44.1	45.7	48.0
	2 P.M.	....	27.603	27.554	27.593	......	56.8	58.9	63.5
	9 P.M.	....	27.595	27.569	27.618	......	47.7	49.1	50.4
	MEAN	....	27.599	27.562	27.608	......	49.5	51.3	54.0
April	7 A.M.	....	27.507	27.523	27.553	......	49.7	46.9	50.4
	2 P.M.	....	27.496	27.524	27.536	......	63.2	59.8	64.3
	9 P.M.	....	27.492	27.535	27.552	......	50.5	49.7	52.4
	MEAN	....	27.498	27.527	27.547	......	54.5	52.1	55.7
May	7 A.M.	....	27.479	27.470	27.418	......	56.0	62.7	59.3
	2 P.M.	....	27.473	27.466	27.423	......	69.0	76.4	74.0
	9 P.M.	....	27.471	27.472	27.427	......	54.9	62.7	60.2
	MEAN	....	27.475	27.469	27.423	......	60.0	67.3	64.5
June	7 A.M.	....	27.494	27.486	27.486	......	70.0	66.5	67.6
	2 P.M.	....	27.484	27.493	27.472	......	86.7	82.4	83.5
	9 P.M.	....	27.493	27.497	27.493	......	69.8	67.9	65.8
	MEAN	....	27.490	27.492	27.484	......	75.5	72.3	72.3
July	7 A.M.	....	27.468	27.473	27.467	......	72.8	72.9	75.9
	2 P.M.	....	27.470	27.468	27.476	......	90.7	89.7	93.3
	9 P.M.	....	27.465	27.476	27.486	......	73.7	73.7	75.4
	MEAN	....	27.468	27.472	27.476	......	79.0	78.8	81.5
August	7 A.M.	....	27.492	27.479	27.494	......	73.9	71.5	70.2
	2 P.M.	....	27.486	27.470	27.488	......	94.4	91.5	88.8
	9 P.M.	....	27.486	27.476	27.504	......	75.7	70.6	69.6
	MEAN	....	27.488	27.475	27.495	......	81.3	77.9	76.2
September	7 A.M.	27.482	27.482	27.518	27.486	61.9	61.6	64.4	65.5
	2 P.M.	27.463	27.464	27.507	27.460	81.8	84.3	82.0	85.8
	9 P.M.	27.475	27.478	27.511	27.482	65.2	65.5	65.3	68.4
	MEAN	27.473	27.475	27.512	27.476	69.6	70.5	70.5	73.2
October	7 A.M.	27.511	27.564	27.569	....	53.2	56.0	57.0	......
	2 P.M.	27.491	27.527	27.548	....	73.0	76.9	76.2	......
	9 P.M.	27.502	27.545	27.571	....	57.8	59.1	59.7	......
	MEAN	27.502	27.545	27.563	....	61.3	64.0	64.3	......
November	7 A.M.	27.618	27.548	27.627	....	46.5	44.5	46.9	......
	2 P.M.	27.594	27.528	27.605	....	62.1	58.3	61.6	......
	9 P.M.	27.611	27.540	27.635	....	50.5	48.1	49.5	......
	MEAN	27.607	27.539	27.622	....	53.0	50.3	52.7	......
December	7 A.M.	27.614	27.576	27.555	....	37.4	44.8	43.4	......
	2 P.M.	27.581	27.556	27.535	....	51.6	55.1	56.6	......
	9 P.M.	27.602	27.553	27.560	....	41.4	48.4	46.2	......
	MEAN	27.599	27.562	27.550	....	43.5	49.4	48.7	......
MEAN OF	7 A.M.	....	27.532	27.536	....	......	54.3	55.2	......
YEAR	2 P.M.	....	27.520	27.527	....	......	70.1	70.2	......
	9 P.M.	....	27.522	27.540	....	......	56.7	57.1	......
GRAND MEAN	......	....	27.525	27.534	....	......	60.4	60.8	......

MONTHLY MEANS OF BAROMETER AND THERMOMETER
AT SUMMIT. (BAROMETER REDUCED TO 32° F.)

Month and Hour.		BAROMETER.				THERMOMETER.			
		1870.	1871.	1872.	1873.	1870.	1871.	1872.	1873.
January	7 A.M.	....	23.302	23.267	23.310	......	22.8	24.9	28.8
	2 P.M.	....	23.289	23.253	23.285	......	34.3	31.0	37.3
	9 P.M.	....	23.300	23.276	23.307	......	25.0	27.8	30.7
	MEAN	....	23.297	23.265	23.301	......	27.4	27.9	32.3
February	7 A.M.	....	23.170	23.180	23.102	......	19.8	29.0	24.6
	2 P.M.	....	23.165	23.187	23.095	......	30.7	32.0	30.0
	9 P.M.	....	23.172	23.190	23.117	......	23.5	30.4	25.8
	MEAN	....	23.169	23.186	23.105	......	24.6	30.5	26.8
March	7 A.M.	....	23.247	23.226	23.308	......	24.9	28.8	30.3
	2 P.M.	....	23.259	23.225	23.292	......	36.0	34.5	40.8
	9 P.M.	....	23.256	23.232	23.314	......	24.6	31.1	33.3
	MEAN	....	23.254	23.228	23.305	......	28.5	31.5	34.8
April	7 A.M.	....	23.194	23.182	23.254	......	33.2	27.2	32.8
	2 P.M.	....	23.195	23.192	23.255	......	42.6	33.6	43.4
	9 P.M.	....	23.204	23.205	23.259	......	28.0	28.5	34.7
	MEAN	....	23.198	23.193	23.256	......	34.6	29.8	37.0
May	7 A.M.	....	23.227	23.265	23.201	......	43.3	40.3	39.0
	2 P.M.	....	23.230	23.265	23.190	......	51.2	49.5	53.8
	9 P.M.	....	23.235	23.264	23.217	......	35.3	40.4	42.1
	MEAN	....	23.231	23.265	23.203	......	43.3	43.4	45.0
June	7 A.M.	....	23.350	23.324	23.325	......	57.8	51.1	47.0
	2 P.M.	....	23.360	23.321	23.305	......	70.1	60.2	59.9
	9 P.M.	....	23.362	23.330	23.323	......	51.1	46.1	51.0
	MEAN	....	23.357	23.325	23.318	......	59.7	52.5	52.6
July	7 A.M.	....	23.368	23.361	23.390	......	56.7	55.4	61.6
	2 P.M.	....	23.367	23.346	23.393	......	71.1	65.5	69.0
	9 P.M.	....	23.364	23.363	23.397	......	53.1	54.3	62.2
	MEAN	....	23.366	23.356	23.393	......	60.3	58.4	64.3
August	7 A.M.	....	23.413	23.341	23.326	......	57.3	51.6	53.9
	2 P.M.	....	23.403	23.324	23.323	......	76.1	66.7	62.7
	9 P.M.	....	23.411	23.343	23.324	......	53.4	52.5	57.7
	MEAN	....	23.409	23.336	23.324	......	62.3	56.9	58.1
September	7 A.M.	23.334	23.343	23.347	....	50.4	52.0	46.3	......
	2 P.M.	23.326	23.331	23.336	....	64.9	65.4	62.5	......
	9 P.M.	23.335	23.343	23.346	....	45.5	45.2	49.9	......
	MEAN	23.332	23.339	23.343	....	53.6	54.2	52.9	......
October	7 A.M.	23.331	23.383	23.365	....	38.7	39.8	41.6	......
	2 P.M.	23.323	23.358	23.337	....	53.4	61.8	56.5	......
	9 P.M.	23.335	23.369	23.354	....	40.8	39.9	43.4	......
	MEAN	23.329	23.370	23.352	....	44.4	47.2	47.2	......
November	7 A.M.	23.359	23.233	23.366	....	29.7	27.1	32.0	......
	2 P.M.	23.339	23.211	23.325	....	43.4	38.6	44.7	......
	9 P.M.	23.358	23.223	23.351	....	32.1	28.6	32.3	......
	MEAN	23.352	23.222	23.347	....	35.1	31.4	36.3	......
December	7 A.M.	23.284	23.240	23.258	....	18.9	27.5	27.2	......
	2 P.M.	23.261	23.214	23.245	....	31.9	35.1	38.0	......
	9 P.M.	23.277	23.226	23.267	....	22.6	30.1	30.4	......
	MEAN	23.274	23.227	23.257	....	24.5	30.9	31.8	......
MEAN OF	7 A.M.	....	23.289	23.290	....	......	38.5	38.0	......
YEAR	2 P.M.	....	23.282	23.280	....	......	51.1	47.9	......
	9 P.M.	....	23.289	23.293	....	......	36.5	38.9	......
GRAND MEAN	......	....	23.287	23.288	....	......	42.0	41.6	......

From what has been said about the observations of the wet-bulb thermometer, taken in connection with the fact that one of the chief objects of the investigation was to prepare a table of corrections to be applied to results obtained in different years and without reference to the element of moisture, it is evident that for purposes of computation the choice lay between the tables of Guyot and those of Williamson, with omission of the portions relating especially to the effect of the vapor in the atmosphere. The observations of the first year, from October, 1870, to September, 1871, were computed by both sets of tables, and the decision reached that Williamson's tables, which make altitudes about four feet in a thousand higher than those of Guyot, give results which, when the means of a long series are used, accord best with the true differences of altitude determined by the spirit-level. With Guyot's tables the errors of midday observations, it is true, are reduced, but those of morning and evening are correspondingly increased. The computations for Tables I.–IX., which form the basis of the subsequent tables of corrections, were all made with aid of Williamson's tables, the correction for temperature in all cases being made by multiplying the first approximate difference of altitude by the sum of the temperatures of the air at the two stations diminished by 64, and then dividing by 900. The corrections for latitude and for decrease of gravity were applied separately in each computation.

Tables I.–III. give the difference of altitude between Sacramento and Colfax, determined barometrically from the mean of the 7 A. M., the 2 P. M., and the 9 P. M. observations as well as from the mean of the day for each month, and from the mean of the year, for the three years from October, 1870, to September, 1873. The difference between the barometric determinations and the true difference of altitude is also shown in the parallel columns. Tables IV.–VI. and VII.–IX. comprise the same data for the stations Sacramento and Summit, and Colfax and Summit respectively. Tables X.–XII., which show the means of these years, were deduced from the preceding tables, and not computed independently from the means of the recorded observations, as it was found from a few trials that the results would be practically identical.

An inspection of these twelve tables leads unmistakably to the following conclusions.

I. *The results are always lower at morning and night than at mid-day.* To this statement there is absolutely no exception.

II. *The results are lower in winter than in summer.* This must also be regarded as universally true, in spite of certain anomalies, for which no complete explanation suggests itself. For instance, in Tables I. and IV., it appears that the 9 P. M. result was actually higher in February, 1871, than in June, July, or August of that year, when the computations were made with reference to Sacramento as the lower station, though the anomaly is less strongly marked in Table VII. for which the lower station was Colfax. In Table II. the 9 P. M. result for December was the highest of the evening results, with one exception, for the whole of the second year; while Tables V. and VIII., which cover the same time as Table II., show the maximum evening result of the whole year in February.

The only explanation that can be offered is, that, in February and December, 1871, there were unusual conditions of the atmosphere prevailing in the valley, and, in February, 1872, upon the mountains. The explanation is far from satisfactory, but it seems impossible to regard the anomalies as due to imperfections in the observations. There is no reason to believe that the observers made any change in the positions of the instruments or exercised less than their ordinary care in observing during those months.

Abnormally high results for both morning and evening appear also in Tables VI. and IX., for the month of February, 1873. The absence of corresponding irregularities in Table III. points again to the mountains as the seat of the disturbance. In fact, the barometer at Summit stood lower for the month of February, 1873, than for any other month during the whole three years; while, both at Sacramento and Colfax, the barometer, though lower than for the same month in the preceding years, was by no means at its minimum.

III. From the two preceding considerations it follows that, as a general rule, *the lower the temperature of the locality, the lower the barometric result, and vice versa.*

IV. *Altitudes determined from daily means approximate most closely to the truth* in February, September, and October between Sacramento and Colfax; that is to say, during the months of transition from one extreme season to the other. Between Sacramento and Summit the best results from daily means are obtained in the summer months, from June to August; while between Colfax and Summit the best daily means are to be expected in March, April, and September.

V. *The mean of the day for points in the foot-hills is much too high during the summer*, though not far from the truth in the winter; but for mountain localities, the station barometer being kept in the valley in both cases, the summer season gives the best approximation, the results in winter being much too low.

VI. *Midday observations give results which are greatly too high all the year round in the valley and foot-hills.* The excess sometimes amounts in summer to more than a hundred feet, and seldom, if ever, falls below twenty-five feet, between Sacramento and Colfax, whose true difference of altitude is only twenty-four hundred feet. Between Sacramento and Summit the results from the 2 P. M. observations were always too high except in the months of December or January, and the excess in one instance amounted to over one hundred and ninety feet. Only once did the result of the two-o'clock observation fall too low between Colfax and Summit, and then by only six feet.

VII. *The 7 A. M. and 9 P. M. observations give results which agree, in the main, with each other.* Both hours give results too low all the year round, almost without exception, between Sacramento and Summit and between Colfax and Summit. In the foot-hills the morning and evening results are generally too high in summer and too low in winter, but the separate years do not show this so clearly as the mean of the three years. In the case of the 7 A. M. observations the discrepancy between barometric measurements and the truth was enormous in winter, amounting in one instance to two hundred and thirty-eight feet between Sacramento and Summit, or about three and one half per cent of the total difference of altitude.

VIII. *The mean of the year* is a little *too high* between Sacramento and Colfax, *too low* between Sacramento and Summit, and quite *near the truth* between Colfax and Summit. The following suggestion is offered as possibly furnishing the key to the explanation of this fact. Owing to the necessary position of the thermometers within only a few feet of the ground, the mean temperature of the air for the year at Summit is probably estimated a little too low, the lowest stratum of air being cooled by the presence and evaporation of the snow. At Colfax, on the other hand, where no snow falls, and where the surface of the earth is intensely heated in summer, the result would naturally be the other way. If these two errors balanced each other exactly, an accurate result might be expected from the yearly means at Colfax and Summit, while the observed discrepancies would show themselves when these two stations were compared respectively with Sacramento.

Tables XIII. – XVI. were prepared from the data contained in the preceding tables for the sake of showing the effect of introducing an intermediate station, part way up the slope, upon the calculated differences of altitude between the valley and points high up on the Sierra. These tables need no detailed explanation. The prominent fact brought to view is that the use of Colfax as an intermediate station increases the calculated difference of altitude between Sacramento and Summit at all seasons of the year and at all hours of the day. For more than two thirds of the time this increase lies between thirty and seventy feet, and may thus be regarded as tolerably constant. The effect of this is to change the times at which the nearest approximations to the truth are to be expected; to increase the error, when the direct measurements are already too high; and to diminish it in cases of the opposite character. The same tables also show incidentally the abnormal character of the results in February, 1873, and, to a less degree, of those in February, 1872, and April, 1873. The minus sign in the column of differences for 2 P. M., Table XV., is an additional proof of the partial untrustworthiness of the Summit record of August, 1873, and justification of the decision to assign a less weight than usual to that month's results.

In Tables XVII. – XIX., which present a comparative view of the results for three years, columns headed " range " have been added in order to show at a glance how measurements made at the same season in different years vary from each other. For Sacramento and Colfax, Table XVII., the range averages less in the winter, from September to March, than in summer; but for Colfax and Summit, Table XIX., the agreement is, on the whole, much better in summer than in winter. The changes from month to month also are, at these seasons, least erratic. The great heat of the summer upon the foot-hills seems to have a greater disturbing influence than the rains of winter; while, when mountain stations alone are considered, the atmosphere in summer is much more uniform from year to year than it is in winter. On Table XVIII., Sacramento and Summit, the range is both larger in amount and more unevenly distributed than on either of the other two tables, which might be reasonably expected from the positions of the stations. In some cases the large variations in successive years arise from obviously anomalous conditions, the nature of which, however, it is not easy to point out; and the practical conclusion to be drawn is, that the longer the observations are continued and the more frequently they are taken each day, the freer the final mean will be from serious errors.

When the data of these tables are represented graphically by curves, it is more clearly evident than it can be from an inspection of the figures alone, that a period of three years even is not long enough, if observations are taken only three times a day, to eliminate all the irregularities incident to the use of the barometer in the Sierra; and that a much better mean curve and a much more probable table of errors will be obtained if the most strikingly obvious discrepancies are not allowed to enter with full force into the mean values. Tables XX.–XXII. are mean tables so made as to represent as nearly as possible the most probable mean values of the errors at different seasons and different hours of the day.

Table XX. was constructed in the following manner. A horizontal line was assumed to represent the true difference of altitude between Sacramento and Colfax, and at equal intervals along this line perpendicular distances were laid off to represent the error of the 7 A. M. observations for each month of each year. The horizontal and vertical scales were so chosen that the curves, which resulted from joining corresponding points, showed very clearly any deviation from regularity. The three curves, thus plotted upon the same sheet of paper, by no means coincided, though the general features presented by each were the same. The curve for the mean of three years was not plotted. The mean curve adopted was a more regular one, drawn with a free hand in such a way as to neutralize, as far as possible, all abnormal irregularities. The proper perpendicular distances of this curve from the horizontal line were then carefully measured on the paper, and the amounts entered in the table as the approximate error of barometric measurements for 7 A. M.

The same course was taken with the other hours and the mean of the day; and similarly for Tables XXI. and XXII. Constructed in this way, these tables are believed to give the best approximation to the truth attainable from the given observations. They show, moreover, in some particulars, more clearly than the first twelve tables, the grounds for the conclusions which have been given above.

To give to the investigation the greatest practical value, it was necessary, furthermore, to prepare a table of corrections, which could be used for observations taken at different hours of the day, and at other points than those specially considered in the discussion, but where the atmospheric conditions might fairly be supposed analogous.

Tables XXIII.–XXV. are of this kind, and give the correction, to be added or subtracted, for each thousand feet of difference of altitude at different hours in the several months. The numbers in heavy-faced type were obtained directly from Tables XX.–XXII. by division, and thus rest upon the foundation of actual observations. The remaining numbers were obtained by the following method of interpolation. The corrections for each month were laid down upon paper in a manner similar to that previously described and the three points joined by a curved line; the season of the year, the times of sunrise and sunset, and the probable rate of change in the value of the correction from morning to noon and from noon to night, being all taken into account. The change in the correction, for instance, was assumed to be most rapid during the hours that the temperature of the air was changing most rapidly, and to be comparatively slight for the two or three hours near the hottest part of the day, and for the hours after sunset. No attempt was made to supply corrections for the night hours, the data not being sufficient for the purpose, and there being no practical use to be made of them.

The most striking fact brought out by a comparison of these three tables with each other is a remarkable difference in the value of the correction for each thousand feet, depending upon the position of the stations. For three o'clock in the afternoon of June, the minus correction amounts to 36.5 feet in a thousand for the foot-hills, and to only 21.6 feet, if the upper station is high in the mountains, — a difference of 14.9 feet. The difference is even greater in the month of December, amounting for 10 A. M. to 19.4 feet. The corrections for the early morning hours also, in Tables XXIV. and XXV., are positive the year round, while in Table XXIII. they are negative from April to September. A partial explanation of these results is to be found in the fact that the temperature of the air in California does not decrease regularly from the sea-level to the summit of the mountains, as it is supposed to do in the development of the barometric formula. In the summer especially the stratum of maximum temperature lies at an altitude of several hundred feet above the valley, though probably not so high as Colfax.

After this description of the tables, it only remains to point out the ways in which they are expected to contribute to the accuracy of barometric work in California, the problem being to make as close an approximation as possible to the real difference of altitude from a single observation or the mean of a short series.

If the observer has it in his power to fix the time of day at which his observation shall be made, or to extend his observations over the whole day, it is easy to see from the tables how he should be guided in the selection of his hours. Or, if the observer is obliged to take his observation at a certain fixed hour, the tables will supply the correction, corresponding to the hour of the day and the season of the year, which will bring the computed result into closer agreement with the truth.

If the points whose altitudes are to be ascertained are in the foothills, and not more than three thousand feet high, the station barometer being observed in the valley at some place not much above the sea-level, Table XXIII. will be the one to use; and the best hours for observing in the different months will be seen at once by inspection. In January, for instance, the closest approximation to the truth is attained between nine and ten in the morning, or from five to seven in the evening. In the month of July nine in the evening is the only hour which gives results requiring little or no correction; but in October the middle of the forenoon and the hours about sunset give equally good results.

A similar use can be made of Table XXIV. for those cases where the station barometer is kept in the valley and the points whose altitudes are desired lie between five and eight thousand feet high. These limits are mentioned, not because they have been determined with accuracy, but because there is every reason to believe that the corrections would have different values if tables similar to these now published could be prepared for the higher altitudes and for some station intermediate between Colfax and Summit. In the measurements of the higher mountain-peaks it will generally be possible to establish a camp or base of reference at some point within the limits to which the published tables apply, and whose absolute altitude can be determined from the mean of observations taken under the most favorable conditions, or by the use of the tabular corrections. For the higher points, then, the principal sources of error would be confined to that portion of the distance which lies above the camp or temporary station; and, in the absence of appropriate tables, the chief dependence must be placed upon the discretion and good judgment of the observer in selecting his times for observation. Had there been any permanently inhabited spot upon the Sierra at a higher elevation than Summit, and one whose absolute altitude could have been ascertained without too great expense, steps would have been taken to collect observations there, with the view of preparing special tables of corrections for the highest points; but the establishment of an independent station upon the mountains for meteorological purposes alone, would have been attended with an expenditure far exceeding the amount of money available for such purposes. It is only upon extensive national surveys, liberally equipped in all respects, that the difficulties can be overcome, and an inquiry of this nature successfully prosecuted. In Colorado, where the Rocky Mountains attain their greatest altitude, it has been possible to run a line of levels to a point over fourteen thousand feet above the level of the sea, and to maintain at this great elevation a permanent station for regular observations, with corresponding ones at lower altitudes, all under the management and control of Professor Hayden and Mr. Gardner, of the Geological Survey of the Territories.

When the mass of material collected at these high stations has been reduced to order, and the necessary computations have been made, it is clear that practical tables of corrections will result, which will be of immediate use in all barometrical work undertaken in the interior of the continent. There will still be a question how far they are applicable to the Sierra Nevada and the mountains of the Pacific coast; but they will certainly indicate whether a greater or less deviation from the truth is to be expected in the higher mountain regions, and what ground there is for the belief that the error of barometric measurements for each thousand feet is less when both barometers are at high altitudes than when the lower one is considerably nearer the level of the sea. That the computed difference of altitude between two high points will vary with the hour of the day at which the observations are taken there can be no doubt; but it seems probable that the daily range of error will be comparatively small, and that a trained observer can so estimate the effects of disturbances in the atmosphere as to select the most favorable point of time for his measurements of the higher peaks. It must also be understood that in California by far the greater number of points, the accurate determination of whose altitude would aid materially in the solution of geological problems, lie at a lower altitude than eight thousand feet; and thus the necessity of extending the investigation to the higher points was less pressing. The exact altitude of the highest peaks, though very desirable to know, cannot be definitely ascertained except with aid of more extended series of observations.

For altitudes between three thousand and five thousand feet, the station of reference being still supposed to be in the valley, there is room for doubt whether Table XXIII. or XXIV. should be recommended. Probably, in the majority of cases, some correction between those given in the two tables would be most near the truth; and the computer should be guided by the general character of the climate of the special district in which the observations are made. If this resembles that of the mountains more than that of the foot-hills a greater weight should be allowed to Table XXIV.; in the opposite case to Table XXIII. Additional observations are needed before this point can be treated more positively.

If the lower station be established at some point between two and three thousand feet high, Table XXV. can be used in the same way as the two preceding; and probably no important error would be introduced by extending its application to altitudes of eight thousand feet or a little more.

Illustrations of the practical use which can be made of the tables are shown in the examples below. They are not selected for any striking peculiarity or for their proving in any extraordinary degree the value of the tables. It happens only that they are the first computations which have been made since the tables were finished, and almost the only cases in which the tabular correction has been applied to any published altitude. The issuing of a new edition of the Yosemite Guide-Book was the occasion of a revision of the principal statements concerning the altitude of important places mentioned, and the opportunity was taken to make an application of the results derived from the labors of the three years. It is not to be expected that the corrections will remedy all the deficiencies of barometric measurements, for it would be seldom the case that the error of any single observation would be just balanced by a correction based upon the mean of a long series. The most that can be looked for is a better agreement among themselves of the altitudes computed from observations taken in different conditions of the atmosphere, and a closer approximation to the truth than would be attained if the corrections were neglected. That these ends are gained is quite evident from the examples cited. The first example is that of the Yosemite Valley.

COMPUTED ALTITUDE OF THE BOTTOM OF YOSEMITE VALLEY.

Date.	Corresponding Station.	A	B	C	D	E	F	G
1867 May 30 7 A.M.	Summit	3042.2	3974.8	+ 18.4	+ 9.0	3051.2	3965.8	+ 18.3
" May 30 2 P.M.	Summit	3081.4	3935.6	− 20.8	− 75.4	3006.0	4011.0	+ 63.5
" June	Sacramento	......	4046.0	+ 89.6	−112.0	......	3934.0	13.5
" Oct.	Sacramento	......	3935.0	− 21.4	+ 34.0	......	3969.0	+ 21.5
1873 July 20 3 P.M.	Sacramento	4002.5	4030.5	+ 74.1	−111.2	3891.3	3919.3	− 28.2
" July 20 3 P.M.	Colfax	1634.0	4061.0	+104.6	− 42.7	1591.3	4018.3	+ 70.8
" July 20 3 P.M.	Summit	3170.4	3846.6	−109.8	− 83.0	3087.4	3929.6	− 17.9
" July 21 7 A.M.	Sacramento	3845.3	3873.3	− 83.1	0	3845.3	3873.3	− 74.1
" July 21 7 A.M.	Colfax	1465.7	3892.7	− 63.7	+ 7.2	1472.9	3899.9	− 47.6
" July 21 7 A.M.	Summit	3048.2	3968.8	+ 12.4	+ 14.4	3062.6	3954.4	+ 6.9

The first column gives the date of the observations in the valley, and the second the station at which corresponding observations were taken. The exact position of the barometer at Summit in 1867 can no longer be determined, but it will be near enough for the present purpose to adopt 7,017 feet as its approximate altitude, though probably that number is a little too small.

Column A contains the computed difference of altitude, uncorrected for the season of the year, between the valley and the respective stations.

Column B contains the different values for the altitude of the valley above the sea, obtained from the results in column A. The mean of column B is 3956.4 feet.

Column C shows the wanderings from the mean of the numbers in B. These cannot be looked upon as representing exactly the errors of the respective measurements, for the absolute altitude of the valley is not known from other than barometrical data. The extreme difference amounts to 214.4 feet.

In column D are given the corrections taken from the new tables, which are to be applied to the numbers in column A. The correction for June, 1867, is based upon the general information that the observations were taken in the middle of the day, and that for October upon the probability that the mean of the day was used by Colonel Williamson, who made the computations.

Columns E and F contain the corrected values of the numbers in A and B. According to these values the altitude of the valley is 3947.5 feet, only 8.9 feet less than the altitude obtained without the use of the corrections. This approach to coincidence is accidental, and speaks neither for nor against the justness of the corrections.

Column G shows the wanderings from the mean of the values in F. These wanderings are still considerable, but the maximum difference has been reduced to 144.9 feet.

On the whole, this example is one of the most unfavorable that could be cited. The Yosemite Valley lies at an altitude of about 3,950 feet above the sea, and thus falls into the doubtful region for which the tables of corrections are not perfectly adapted; and, besides, it must be allowed that observations taken upon the narrow strip of comparatively level land which lies between the nearly vertical bounding walls of the valley would naturally be more or less affected by the physical peculiarities of the place.

The two following cases will be seen to show the worth of the new tables in a more favorable light. The different columns are designated in the same way as the corresponding columns in the example just given.

For the Tuolumne Cañon the use of the corrections has reduced the computed altitude from 7809.6, the mean of column B, to 7770.2 feet, the mean of column F; and the maximum difference between any two results has fallen from 323.3 to 167.5 feet; that is to say, by not quite fifty per cent, though more than in the case of the Yosemite Valley.

COMPUTED ALTITUDE OF CAMP IN TUOLUMNE CAÑON, NEAR VIRGINIA PASS TRAIL.

Date.	Corresponding Station.	A	B	C	D	E	F	G
1873 July 28 7 A.M.	Sacramento	7603.3	7631.3	−178.3	+ 87.4	7690.7	7718.7	−51.5
" July 28 7 A.M.	Colfax	5281.2	7708.2	−101.4	+ 29.5	5310.7	7737.7	−32.5
" July 28 1 P.M.	Sacramento	7907.1	7935.1	+125.5	−130.6	7776.5	7804.5	+34.3
" July 28 1 P.M.	Colfax	5527.6	7954.6	+145.0	−145.3	5382.3	7809.3	+39.1
" July 29 7 A.M.	Sacramento	7735.9	7763.9	− 45.7	+ 88.6	7824.5	7852.5	+82.3
" July 29 7 A.M.	Colfax	5228.5	7655.5	−154.1	+ 29.5	5258.0	7685.0	−85.2
" July 29 1 P.M.	Sacramento	7902.6	7930.6	+121.0	−130.6	7772.0	7800.0	+29.8
" July 29 1 P.M.	Colfax	5471.0	7898.0	+ 88.4	−144.0	5327.0	7754.0	−16.2

The effect of the corrections for Peregoy's is to reduce the extreme difference from 96.1 to 13.1 feet, a larger reduction than could be hoped for in the great majority of cases. The computed altitude, 6978.0 feet, has been in this case increased to 7000.4 feet.

COMPUTED ALTITUDE OF PEREGOY'S.

Date.	Corresponding Station.	A	B	C	D	E	F	G
1873 July 19 7 P.M.	Sacramento	6959.7	6987.7	+ 9.7	+ 12.6	6972.3	7000.3	− 0.1
" July 19 7 P.M.	Colfax	4594.7	7021.7	+ 43.7	− 14.0	4580.7	7007.7	+ 7.3
" July 20 7 A.M.	Sacramento	6897.6	6925.6	− 52.4	+ 69.0	6966.6	6994.6	− 5.8
" July 20 7 A.M.	Colfax	4550.2	6977.2	− 0.8	+ 21.6	4571.8	6998.8	− 1.6

In these examples the exhibit is made the more unfavorable, because, in nearly every instance, single observations have been computed independently, and the wandering of each one from the mean shown. If a different course had been followed, and the mean of the two successive mornings, for instance, in the Tuolumne Cañon, been taken as the probable morning average, the result would have given stronger evidence of the usefulness and necessity of applying the corrections from the new tables. To show this more clearly the following table is added, in which the mean of the results for two successive days is given for each of the hours.

COMPUTED ALTITUDE OF CAMP IN TUOLUMNE CAÑON.

Mean of two days.

Date.	Corresponding Station.	Uncorrected.		Corrected.	
1873 July, 7 A.M.	Sacramento	7697.6	−112.0	7785.6	+ 15.4
July, 7 A.M.	Colfax	7681.8	−127.8	7711.3	− 58.9
July, 1 P.M.	Sacramento	7932.9	+123.3	7802.3	+ 32.1
July, 1 P.M.	Colfax	7926.3	+116.7	7781.6	+ 11.4

The reduction of the maximum variation is consequently from 251.1 to 91.0 feet, or nearly 64 per cent.

Any higher degree of accuracy in the determination of altitudes than that illustrated by the examples now given seems scarcely attainable by the use of the barometer, unless the observations can be continued for a considerable time at the two points whose difference of altitude is wished; and not even then, unless attention be paid to the season of the year and the hours of the day at which the observations are taken. But when these precautions are observed and the proper allowance is made for the special circumstances attending each case, there is no doubt that the barometer furnishes the readiest means of ascertaining the altitudes of elevated points, with little labor and only moderate expense, to within very narrow limits of error.

It is, in fact, indispensable upon surveys in wild and mountainous regions, if the estimates of heights are to be anything better than guesswork. The use of the spirit-level, or similar instrument of precision, would be entirely out of the question, not merely from the attendant expenses and the amount of time required to run the lines, but also from the difficulty of carrying the instrument up the steepest slopes, where oftentimes even the barometer strapped to the back begins to be a serious hindrance to progress in the ascent. It needs, perhaps, to be dwelt upon with more than usual emphasis in this place, after what has been written of the imperfections of this method of measurement, that the barometer, for purposes of hypsometry, holds a position peculiarly its own.

It can make no claim to unfailing accuracy, but, when used with judgment and with proper attention to details of time and place, it gives results which are very near the truth, and which cannot be reached by any other means at the command of the surveyor or explorer. The object of the present discussion is not to weaken confidence in barometric work, but to show in what way it may be carried on so as to yield the best results and contribute the most trustworthy information about some of the most prominent features in the physical geography of the elevated regions of the globe.

For points whose difference of altitude is not great, however, no very close approximation to the truth ought to be expected, particularly if the stations lie on opposite sides of mountain ranges and show any marked dissimilarity of climate. This will appear very strikingly from an examination of the following table, which shows the computed difference of altitude between the barometer at Mr. Freeman's house on L Street, Sacramento, and the station barometer at No. 91 Montgomery Block, San Francisco, for the first seven months of the year 1871, the only period, during the three years covered by the investigation, at which observations could be kept up with regularity at the San Francisco office of the Survey. The observer for these seven months was Mr. Charles Rabe. The barometer at San Francisco was known to be twenty-eight feet above that at Sacramento. The table also shows the deviation of the computed results from the truth.

COMPUTED ALTITUDE OF NO. 91 MONTGOMERY BLOCK, SAN FRANCISCO,
ABOVE L STREET, SACRAMENTO.

Date.		7 A. M.		2 P. M.		9 P. M.		Mean.	
1871	January	57.3	+29.3	47.7	+19.7	35.3	+ 7.3	46.9	+18.9
	February	44.8	+16.8	49.7	+21.7	38.1	+10.1	43.6	+15.6
	March	29.0	+ 1.0	38.2	+10.2	13.8	−14.2	26.7	− 1.3
	April	19.1	− 8.9	18.7	− 9.3	3.7	−24.3	13.9	−14.1
	May	19.3	− 8.7	7.4	−20.6	9.2	−18.8	12.2	−15.8
	June	2.9	−25.1	− 5.7	−33.7	−20.6	−48.6	− 8.5	−36.5
	July	− 4.7	−32.7	−20.2	−48.2	−25.3	−53.3	−16.0	−44.0

The effect of the heat in the Sacramento Valley in expanding the air and diminishing the pressure, so that the barometer stands uniformly lower, though actually nearer the sea-level, at Sacramento than at San Francisco during midsummer, is made very manifest by the minus signs in the results for June and July. Were there no other sources of information than barometric observations in these months, it would be admitted by every one that the streets of Sacramento must stand at a higher level than the upper stories of high buildings on Montgomery Street, San Francisco. The cause of this is to be looked for chiefly in the extraordinary differences in the range of temperature at the two places. For the seven months in question the lowest recorded temperature at San Francisco was 42°.3, January 12, 7 A. M.; and the highest, 75°, June 6, 2 P. M. At Sacramento the range was from 31°, January 11, 7 A. M., to 101°.5, June 29, 2 P. M., — more than double the extreme variation at San Francisco.

The tables of corrections whose construction and use have now been described will not, of course, be strictly applicable for cases which fall entirely outside the limits for which they were calculated. Could similar tables, based upon observations in other countries or other parts of this country, be brought side by side with these for comparison, there would doubtless be in all instances a general similarity in the main features, accompanied by such decided differences in the numerical values of the corrections, that no single table could be adopted for universal use. * For the sake of illustrating these differences the two following tables are added to give an idea of what might have been expected if San Francisco instead of Sacramento had been chosen for the lower station of reference.

SAN FRANCISCO AND COLFAX.
True difference of altitude 2371 feet.

Date.		7 A. M.		2 P. M.		9 P. M.		Mean.	
1871	January	2322.3	−48.7	2382.6	+11.6	2343.9	−27.1	2349.4	−21.6
	February	2349.0	−22.0	2385.4	+14.4	2376.5	+ 5.5	2370.5	− 9.5
	March	2375.5	+ 4.5	2408.9	+37.9	2382.5	+11.5	2389.0	+18.0
	April	2375.2	+ 4.2	2422.1	+51.1	2376.5	+ 5.5	2391.1	+20.1
	May	2399.7	+28.7	2443.3	+72.3	2391.2	+20.2	2411.3	+40.3
	June	2393.4	+22.4	2448.2	+77.2	2378.9	+ 7.9	2407.4	+36.4
	July	2410.9	+39.9	2455.2	+84.2	2396.1	+25.1	2420.0	+49.0

* Compare Chapter III., page 63.

SAN FRANCISCO AND SUMMIT.

True difference of altitude 6961 feet.

Date.	7 A. M.		2 P. M.		9 P. M.		Mean.	
1871 January	6799.0	−162.0	6930.2	−30.8	6837.1	−123.9	6855.5	−105.5
February	6871.4	− 89.6	6999.4	+38.4	6909.6	− 51.4	6927.0	− 34.0
March	6906.2	− 54.8	7018.7	+57.7	6902.8	− 58.2	6942.9	− 18.1
April	6930.8	− 30.2	7038.0	+77.0	6872.2	− 88.8	6946.6	− 14.4
May	6956.7	− 4.3	7047.5	+86.5	6878.7	− 82.3	6961.2	+ 0.2
June	6901.1	− 59.9	7016.2	+55.2	6827.4	−133.6	6915.9	− 45.1
July	6855.2	−105.8	6993.5	+32.5	6817.7	−143.3	6888.8	− 72.2

The series is so short that a detailed discussion of its peculiar features is unnecessary and would lead to no practical results, and it is to be regretted that the material is not at hand for comparing the results of an entire year. The chief points of interest will be detected at once by a comparison with Tables I. and IV., portions of which relate to the same period of time.

CHAPTER III.

RÉSUMÉ OF SIMILAR INVESTIGATIONS OUTSIDE OF CALIFORNIA.

IN the introductory chapter a condensed account has been given of the principal modifications which have been made, or proposed, in the barometric formula, for the sake of bringing the results obtained by its use into a closer agreement with the truth. It is there mentioned that the occurrence of unexpectedly large discrepancies in the heights of important points, when the measurements are made in different seasons of the year, or in different conditions of the atmosphere of whatever nature, has attracted the attention of observers from time to time; and it is further shown that no change in the formula has been able to remedy the difficulty entirely. Improved determinations of the values of the constant factors, and, for computations based upon extended series of observations, the introduction of a special term for the effect of the aqueous vapor in the atmosphere, added, it is true, to the degree of accuracy attainable and reduced the discrepancies in part; but the differences in the results still remained too great to be explained solely as errors of observation, and were of such a nature that they could not properly be charged to deficiencies in the formula.

It is the object of the present chapter to give in a concise form a comparative view of the principal suggestions which have been made for eliminating or avoiding these residual errors, and to show that the method followed in the California investigation is the one which leads most directly to practical results, and upon which the chief dependence is to be placed.

As early as 1806, Ramond* published a memoir in which he attributed

---

* Mémoires, etc., pp. 39 – 59.

the discordance of results obtained by different observers to the influence
of the hour of the day, the influence of locality, and the influence of the
winds and air-currents. The change from hour to hour, or the daily variation, he considered the most important, and proved its existence by citing
the means of altitudes computed from observations taken at different hours
from six in the morning to ten at night at Bagnères and at Barèges, when
compared with synchronous observations taken by Dangos at Tarbes. His
comments upon the observed facts, almost literally translated, are as follows : —

"Seven or eight hundred observations of this kind, each calculated
separately, have shown constantly the same sort of variation. The seasons
of the year and the differences of locality have introduced no changes
except in the range of the variation. At the tops of mountains, on plains,
or in the depths of valleys, observations in the forenoon and the afternoon
have led to results which are smaller just in proportion to the length of
time between midday and the actual moment of observation; although
it is not precisely at the hour of noon that the maximum results are
found. The computed altitudes continue increasing until towards one or
two o'clock, a little earlier or a little later; but both the amount of the
increase and the time of reaching the maximum depend largely upon the
season of the year, the clearness of the day, and perhaps the direction
of the wind. A small part of this daily variation can be attributed to the
hygrometric state of the atmosphere, and it would not be difficult to introduce into the calculation a correction for the humidity of the air; but
the largest part of the error results, without doubt, from a cause much
more powerful and much more difficult to estimate; to wit, the influence
of ascending and descending currents of air which act both upon the
barometer and thermometer, either in diminishing or increasing the weight
of the air-column, according to their velocity and direction, or in bringing
from an upper or lower region a temperature which does not belong by
right to the place where the observation is made. Such disturbances are
essentially anomalous, ... and there is no other resource than to avoid
the hours where their interference is most common. The hours of the
middle of the day are the least affected, and among these the hour of
noon has this particular advantage, that the heights which it gives are
sufficiently near the mean of those which are obtained from observations

made within the limits of three or four hours which are included in the short period of equilibrium."

As to the influence of locality, Ramond advises that the barometer should be observed, when possible, upon the summit of isolated peaks; for the more complete the isolation the less will the observations be affected by local causes of disturbance. In particular, he shows the comparative untrustworthiness of the barometer as an instrument for determining small differences of altitude in level countries.

The discussion of the influence of the winds was taken up by Ramond at considerable length, and the conclusion reached that the computed heights would be too high when the wind blew strongly from the north, and too low when strong southerly winds prevailed.

In a subsequent memoir, published in 1808, Ramond appears to have made a partial study of the annual variation in barometric measurements, without dwelling upon it in much detail. He says:* "Experience has taught me that each month and each season exercises its influence upon the instruments. It was natural to look upon the revolution of the four seasons as a cycle, in which the greater part of the compensations would manifest themselves, and I have become convinced that the space of a year cannot be arbitrarily lengthened or shortened, without making the distinctive character of the particular season predominate in the result." Under Ramond's direction observations were taken at noon of each day, with only occasional omissions, for two years at Clermont, in Central France, and at Paris. The observations began in 1806, and closed in 1808. The observations were computed separately, and the means for each month, translated into English measure, are given in the table below.

COMPUTED DIFFERENCE OF ALTITUDE BETWEEN PARIS AND CLERMONT.

January	1110.3	+ 13.9	July	1112.9	+ 16.5
February	1031.5	− 64.9	August	1128.3	+ 31.9
March	1157.2	+ 60.8	September	1103.4	+ 7.0
April	1127.6	+ 31.2	October	1106.3	+ 9.9
May	1107.0	+ 10.6	November	1046.9	− 49.5
June	1145.4	+ 49.0	December	980.3	− 116.1

* Mémoires, etc., p. 71.

The mean value for the year, 1096.4 feet, was adopted as the true difference of altitude between the two stations. The table shows decided differences in the different months, and the average for the six months of spring and summer is over sixty-five feet more than the average for the six months of autumn and winter, but the change from month to month is not so regular as might have been expected; and Ramond, probably on account of this irregularity, did not publish any directions which relate to the best season of the year in which to make measurements.

In the concluding remarks to his third memoir he says:* "Results as satisfactory as they have been unexpected have been the reward of my labor. I have seen a wonderful agreement established between the changes of the atmosphere and the errors which appeared at first anomalous; I have seen the one serve as an index and sometimes as a measure of the other, and all reduced to a small number of general effects, which themselves spring from a common cause; and now a very simple and homogeneous theory binds, in my mind, all the phenomena together. The surface of the atmosphere tends constantly to a level form, and the weight of the air-columns varies with the changes which take place in the density of their strata. Variations in temperature are the principal cause of these changes of density. Every change of temperature causes a wind or springs from a wind, which conveys from one place to another the temperature and density which it received at its origin. These currents of air can have only three directions with respect to the surface of the earth: they are vertical, inclined, or horizontal. When they assume the latter direction, they act by the difference which exists between their density and that of the layers they replace. When they follow one of the first two directions, the effect of the velocity of ascent or descent is combined with that of the density."

The words of Ramond have been thus freely quoted because they contain the first clear statement of the existence of a diurnal period in barometric measurements. The similar observations made by Deluc in the previous century had rested upon a poorer foundation, and the low results obtained at sunrise were thought by him to be caused by the easterly

* Mémoires, etc., pp. 116–119.

winds prevailing at that hour; for, when the wind blew from any other direction, the discrepancy was less.* Ramond's belief that observations at noon were in all cases the most to be relied upon, and his advice to confine them entirely to that hour, would, if adopted, materially abridge the usefulness of the barometer upon geological and topographical surveys; for it is not generally in the power of the explorer to be upon the spot whose altitude is wished at just the hour of noon, and, besides, it is now well understood that neither that hour nor any other will give the best approximation in all the months.

That there is an annual as well as a diurnal variation was pointed out by D'Aubuisson† much more satisfactorily than by Ramond. The difference of altitude between Geneva and St. Bernard, computed from the mean of the two-o'clock observations for the four years from 1818 to 1821, was least in the month of December, and increased without interruption until June, in which month it was at its maximum; it then decreased with equal regularity until December. The wandering from the mean value amounted in December to 79, and in June to 92 feet, making the extreme discrepancy 171 feet. These numbers are very much greater than those in the table given in the introductory chapter, page 24; but it must be remembered that those results came from means of the day and not from the means of midday alone. The more modern formulæ, also, make the range of error between summer and winter less than the older ones; so that the difference between the two cases is really less than might be expected, if anything is to be allowed for the improvements in the construction of instruments in the thirty or forty years intervening. D'Aubuisson explains both the diurnal and the annual variation, not by ascending and descending currents of air, as Ramond did, but by the error in the estimation of the actual mean temperature of the air-column when this is taken to be the half-sum of the extreme temperatures, and adds: "From what has just been said it follows that our temperature term will err in excess: firstly, at those hours or moments of the day

---

* See Suckow's Barometrische Hypsometrie. Darmstadt, 1843. p. 51.

† D'Aubuisson's Traité de Géognosie, Paris, 1828, Tom. I. p. 495. The same topic was discussed by him more briefly at earlier dates in contributions to the Bibliothèque Universelle and other periodicals.

when the temperature at the surface of the earth rises above the mean value, and so much the more in amount the more rapid or considerable the rise is; secondly, when, from one day to another, a notable elevation of temperature prevails; thirdly, in the hottest season of the year." But he despaired of being able to separate from other errors of observation those which belonged to the temperature term alone, and confined himself to certain comments " which should give an idea of the influence of these variations of temperature from hour to hour, from day to day, and from season to season." This was valuable as far as it went, and served as a tolerable measure of the degree of accuracy attainable in the use of the barometer, but was not expected to lead to any systematic application of corrections.

The diurnal variation in barometric measurements was also made a subject of investigation by Horner, of Zurich, one of the companions of Krusenstern in his voyage around the world, and to whom so much credit is due for his contributions to Swiss geography. As early as 1813, his attention had been called to the subject, but it was not until fourteen years later that he was able to make the necessary observations under favorable conditions. In August, 1827, he published a paper * in which was given in detail an account of the determination of the height of the Righi above Zurich, both trigonometrically and barometrically. Between the 22d of January and the 1st of February, 1827, 118 synchronous observations at Zurich and upon the top of the mountain were obtained, and each computed by itself. The difference of altitude from the mean of observations at 7 A. M. was 4161.6 feet, and the increase was regular and unbroken until 1 P. M., for which hour the computed difference was 4221.6 feet. The extreme variation, therefore, between early morning and midday amounted to about $\frac{1}{70}$ of the total height, hardly more than half the amount of variation for the corresponding month and hours in California, as will appear from a glance at Tables X. – XII.

The work was taken up again in June of the same year, and 166 synchronous observations made between the 2d and the 17th of the month. The rise from morning to midday and the fall from midday to evening were

---

* Denkschriften der allgemeinen Schweizerischen Gesellschaft für Naturwissenschaften. Band 1, Zürich, 1833, Abtheilung 2, pp. 137 – 174.

even more regular than in January, but the amount of variation was different, being only $\frac{1}{85}$ instead of $\frac{1}{70}$, and the maximum value was given as early as 11 A. M. The amount of variation between morning and noon was found by Ramond in the Pyrenees to amount to as much as $\frac{1}{48}$ of the total difference of altitude.[*]

A comparison of these two sets of results showed that in summer the mean of all the observations gave a result higher by 45.6 feet than the mean of the winter observations. For this difference Horner suggested several possible explanations, prominent among which was an erroneous estimate of the effect of the aqueous vapor in the atmosphere; but he reached no satisfactory conclusion, and proposed at that time no means of overcoming the difficulty. For the true difference of altitude between Zurich and the Righi he depended upon trigonometrical measurements. With these the barometric results for the winter season agreed in the middle of the day; but in summer the hours just after sunrise or before sunset gave the most accurate results. In view of these inequalities, Horner pointed out the great danger of error in making barometric measurements, or in attempting to improve the coefficients of the formula, if dependence was placed upon observations taken without any regard to times or seasons. The best course to be followed was also indicated by him in nearly the following words: "From these series of observations there seems to be proved the necessity of a horary correction, and possibly of one other, which shall depend upon the deviations of the observed temperatures from the mean temperature of the place." The results under discussion not furnishing sufficient data, the further development of this idea had to be postponed. That it was not abandoned is proved by his having left among his papers a table of corrections for different hours of the day to be applied to the computed differences of altitude. The observations upon which these corrections were based are not known, but the table is printed in part by Bravais,[†] by whom it was seen at Zurich in 1842. The original table was too long to be quoted entire, but the portion available and given on the next page is enough to show the line of thought upon which Horner was engaged. It will be observed that no

[*] Suckow's Barometrische Hypsometrie, p. 56.

[†] Comptes Rendus, Tom. XXXI., 1850, p. 176.

reference is here made to the season of the year, and that the correction for the hour of the day, whether positive or negative, increases much more rapidly than the altitude, — a point which does not seem to have been well established by later observations. In the original table the heights and corrections are all given in toises.

CORRECTIONS TO BE APPLIED TO THE COMPUTED HEIGHTS.

Height.	12 M.	1 P. M.	2 P. M.	3 P. M.	4 P. M.	5 P. M.	6 P. M.
200	− 0.6	− 0.4	− 0.3	− 0.1	+ 0.1	+ 0.3	+ 0.5
400	− 1.4	− 1.1	− 0.7	− 0.2	− 0.1	+ 0.6	+ 1.1
600	− 2.4	− 1.8	− 1.3	− 0.4	+ 0.2	+ 1.1	+ 2.0
800	− 3.7	− 2.8	− 2.0	− 0.6	+ 0.3	+ 1.7	+ 3.1
1000	− 5.2	− 4.0	− 2.8	− 0.8	+ 0.5	+ 2.3	+ 4.4
1200	− 7.0	− 5.4	− 3.7	− 1.1	+ 0.7	+ 3.2	+ 5.8

The horary correction proposed by Bravais himself, from an examination of the observations of De Saussure and of Kaemtz, were as follows: —

At noon subtract $\frac{1}{97}$ of the height.

" 1 P. M. " $\frac{1}{95}$ " "

" 2 " " $\frac{1}{103}$ " "

" 3 " " $\frac{1}{125}$ " "

" 4 " " $\frac{1}{173}$ " "

" 5 " " $\frac{1}{300}$ " "

" 6 " " $\frac{1}{1000}$ " "

The absence of any reference to the season of the year makes this table valueless for general use, though it served the special purpose for which it was made by Bravais.

The investigations of Kaemtz in the Alps during his journeyings there in 1832 [*] also reached no further than the diurnal variation, as no attention could be paid to the annual variation on account of the shortness of the time given up to taking observations. The points at which he made the most complete series of observations were the Righi and the Faulhorn; referring in one case to both Zurich and Geneva, and in the other to Zurich alone. His method of ascertaining the true value of the correction

* Poggendorff's Annalen der Physik und Chemie, Band 27, 1833, pp. 345 – 361.

for each hour of the day and night was more general than the others which have been referred to. He employed an interpolation formula of the form which is commonly used in meteorological investigations, where the effects of periodicity in any disturbing cause are to be estimated. Letting x denote the mean value of the separate hourly results, or the true difference of altitude, and X_n the true result for the nth hour after noon, the formula takes the form,

$$X_n = x + a \sin (n\ 15° + a) + b \sin (2\ n\ 15° + \beta) + c \sin (3\ n\ 15° + \gamma),$$

where a, b, c, are numerical coefficients and a, β, γ, auxiliary angles, whose values are to be determined so as to make the results calculated from this formula agree with the observed results for those hours at which observations were actually taken. The formula will then hold for all values of n from 1 to 24, that is, for every hour of day and night, and can be used for purposes of interpolation and for ascertaining the times at which the computed altitudes are at their maximum, minimum, or mean values. Between Zurich and the Righi the maximum was found to fall about half past eleven in the forenoon, thus agreeing quite closely with Horner, and the minimum at three o'clock in the morning. The mean or true value was obtainable at quarter past seven in the morning or at seven in the evening. The difference between the maximum and the minimum values amounted to about $\frac{1}{56}$ of the total difference of altitude.

Similar calculations for Zurich and the Faulhorn led to slightly different results. The hour of the maximum altitude was ten minutes before one in the afternoon, and of the minimum, quarter past four in the morning. The extreme variation amounted to $\frac{1}{42}$ of the true elevation of the mountain above Zurich.

With the assistance of a formula of this kind it would be possible to prepare quite full tables of corrections, but it does not appear that that was any part of the purpose which Kaemtz had in view; and even if such a table had been made, its measure of trustworthiness would be just equal to that of the observations on which it was based, and its application be restricted to the mountains of Switzerland. Without going further into the details of the facts upon which Kaemtz founded his opinion, it may be added that he believed the source of the errors to lie in the incorrect estimation of the real mean temperature of the air-column, when this is assumed to be equal to the half-sum of the two temperatures observed at the extreme stations.

The formula proposed by General Baeyer, as has been mentioned on page 21, gave results which reduced in some measure the extreme variation between morning and midday, but not entirely. His published observations cover only a part of one day, September 1, 1849, but they were taken hourly, and were computed by Laplace's formula as well as by his own, so that the comparative value of the two formulæ is clearly shown. Between Kupferkuhle and the Brocken, in the Hartz Mountains, whose difference of altitude, ascertained trigonometrically, was 2,989 feet, the extreme variation arising from the use of Laplace's formula was 66.7, and from Baeyer's, 58.4 feet; a gain too slight to inspire much confidence in the proposed new form for the temperature term. Baeyer's advice to observers is to take the mean of observations between ten in the morning and half past five in the afternoon as the best approximation to the truth, because the results obtained before ten o'clock or later than half past five are too low. One of the most interesting parts of Baeyer's paper shows that the same causes which produce the diurnal variation in the barometer exert a like influence, though in the opposite direction, upon altitudes determined trigonometrically, the morning results being too high and those of midday being too low.

The meteorological observations which have been taken at Geneva and St. Bernard have furnished abundant material for a much more thorough study of the general subject of barometric measurements than has been possible in any of the cases previously referred to; and the admirable memoir by Professor Plantamour,* in which he discusses the results derived from the mean of the ten years from 1841 to 1850, has been more frequently quoted than any similar paper in the recent history of the barometer. Ten years was a period long enough to eliminate nearly if not quite all the anomalies which might manifest themselves in any single year, and to give an excellent mean value for the computed heights in each month. In spite of all precautions and of the use of a special humidity correction the change from month to month proves to be nearly as great as when

---

* Mémoires de la Société de Physique et d'Histoire Naturelle de Genève, Tom. XIII., 1852, pp. 1 – 62.

the calculations are made according to the original formula of Laplace. Plantamour's suspicions, as those of nearly all previous observers, fell upon the method employed for getting the mean temperature, and he says that the largest part of the discrepancies in barometric measurements is chargeable to the assumption "that the mean temperature of the air-column between the two stations is equal to the half-sum of the temperatures at the two extremities." The proper step to take, therefore, is to apply some correction to the temperature, determined in the ordinary way, so as to make it approximate more closely to the truth; for the true mean "is equal to the half-sum of the temperatures observed at the two extremities, plus a certain correction, which varies with the hour of the day, with the season of the year, and from accidental causes."

To ascertain the value of this correction, Plantamour reversed the computations for altitude, and, taking the heights of the barometers and the true difference of altitude as the known quantities, regarded the temperature correction, or the true mean temperature, as the quantity to be determined. Having in this way found what he considered to be the true temperature of the mass of air for the different hours of the day in each month, it required only a simple subtraction to know what correction ought to have been applied to the observed temperatures at each hour, to bring them into accord with the true temperature. These corrections he arranged in a tabular form, and showed that they varied less from month to month than from hour to hour in the same month. The least values of the correction for the mean of the day are found in March and September, which months are accordingly recommended as best suited for measuring altitudes barometrically. In July the altitudes are too high, excepting between midnight and four o'clock in the morning, and in December they are all too low, without exception.

By multiplying each number in Plantamour's table by a constant quantity, equal to the increase in the computed heights caused by an increase of one degree in the assumed value of the mean temperature, a table similar in form to Tables XX. – XXII. of the California series can be prepared. Such a table has, in fact, been made, and was included by Guyot * in his

---

* Tables, Meteorological and Physical, prepared for the Smithsonian Institution, Washington, 1859, Series D, p. 82.

collection. It would be easy to translate this into English measures, and find how much the correction for each thousand feet would amount to, but no practical gain would ensue, for the table, even in that form, would not be adapted for use in California.

The same set of observations were also studied independently by Lieutenant H. L. Renny, during a residence in Switzerland in 1857; and a very valuable memoir, entitled "On the Constants of the Barometric Formulæ which make correct allowance for the Hygrometric State of the Atmosphere," although by far the larger part of the paper is taken up with the discussion of the subject of the horary correction, was read by him before the Irish Academy in the following year.* Plantamour's table of corrections, above referred to, is shown by Renny to be defective, because the correct height of the Convent of Saint Bernard above the Observatory of Geneva, determined by an accurate survey with the spirit-level, was not known until after the table had been published. Renny's own table of horary corrections is more complete than that of Plantamour, and was prepared in almost precisely the same way as that chosen for the California investigation.† He says: "I made no less than two hundred and eighty-eight distinct calculations for every hour, night and day, of every month of the year. . . . . Then subtracting each calculated height from the true height, as ascertained by accurate spirit-levelling, ... the error of each calculated height is known. Such error, being divided by the calculated height, gives the horary correction; for if such horary correction be multiplied by the calculated height, we necessarily have the difference of calculated and true height; and such difference, being added to or subtracted from the calculated height, according to the sign of the horary correction, necessarily gives the true height."

The table given by Renny is arranged in a different form from that

<hr/>

* Transactions of the Royal Irish Academy, Vol. XXIII., 1859, pp. 623 – 668.

† Lieutenant Renny's treatment of the subject of special barometric corrections came near being overlooked entirely in the search made for memoirs of this character, on account of the incomplete title of his paper. The use of any formula involving a separate correction for moisture having been found impracticable upon the California work, the paper of Renny's was not read until some time in April, 1874, after all the tables prepared for California had been finished and electrotyped, and it was then examined without the expectation of finding anything which bore upon the immediate subject in hand.

adopted in this work, and supplies a correction for every hour, day and night, for every month of the year. A portion of that table, so transformed as to be directly comparable with Table XXIV. and comprising only the hours from 7 A. M. to 9 P. M., is given below. The mean of twenty-four hours has been given in preference to the mean of the morning, midday, and evening correction, which would be in some respects better for purposes of comparison.

CORRECTIONS TO BE APPLIED FOR EACH THOUSAND FEET BETWEEN GENEVA AND SAINT BERNARD.

Hour.	Jan.	Feb.	Mar.	April.	May.	June.	July.	Aug.	Sept.	Oct.	Nov.	Dec.
7 A.M.	+8.7	+8.4	+ 5.6	+ 1.3	− 0.8	− 1.8	− 2.0	+ 0.6	+4.5	+6.5	+10.1	+12.5
8 "	+7.3	+6.2	+ 1.7	− 2.5	− 4.8	− 5.5	− 5.9	− 3.5	+0.8	+3.7	+ 8.2	+11.2
9 "	+5.5	+3.2	− 2.3	− 6.5	− 8.4	− 8.8	− 9.3	− 7.2	−2.6	+0.9	+ 5.8	+ 9.5
10 "	+3.5	+0.2	− 5.8	− 9.7	−11.4	−11.3	−11.9	− 9.8	−5.4	−1.7	+ 3.4	+ 7.5
11 "	+2.0	−2.4	− 8.4	−11.9	−13.1	−13.2	−13.8	−11.6	−7.5	−3.6	+ 1.5	+ 5.6
12 M.	+0.4	−4.1	− 9.7	−12.9	−13.8	−14.1	−14.6	−12.4	−8.4	−4.5	+ 0.1	+ 4.3
1 P.M.	0	−4.6	−10.0	−12.9	−13.5	−14.3	−14.8	−12.5	−8.6	−4.7	− 0.4	+ 3.8
2 "	+0.4	−4.0	− 9.0	−11.6	−12.4	−13.8	−14.2	−11.8	−7.9	−4.0	+ 0.4	+ 4.2
3 "	+1.4	−2.5	− 7.0	− 9.8	−10.7	−12.6	−12.8	−10.6	−6.5	−2.6	+ 1.7	+ 5.3
4 "	+2.7	−0.5	− 4.6	− 7.2	− 8.6	−10.8	−11.1	− 8.9	−4.7	−0.9	+ 3.3	+ 6.8
5 "	+4.7	+1.8	− 2.0	− 4.7	− 5.8	− 8.3	− 8.6	− 6.7	−2.6	+1.0	+ 5.0	+ 8.3
6 "	+6.1	+3.7	+ 0.3	− 2.2	− 3.3	− 5.6	− 6.1	− 4.3	−0.6	+2.9	+ 6.3	+ 9.7
7 "	+7.0	+5.3	+ 2.4	− 0.1	− 0.6	− 2.8	− 3.6	− 2.0	+1.3	+4.6	+ 7.4	+10.7
8 "	+7.6	+6.3	+ 4.1	+ 1.7	+ 1.7	− 0.3	− 1.1	0	+2.8	+6.1	+ 8.1	+11.1
9 "	+7.8	+7.1	+ 5.3	+ 3.2	+ 3.6	+ 2.1	+ 0.8	+ 1.7	+4.0	+7.4	+ 8.5	+11.2
Mean of 24 Hours.	+6.2	+4.7	+ 2.0	− 0.8	− 1.2	− 2.5	− 3.3	− 1.4	+1.3	+4.3	+ 6.9	+ 9.6

Table XXIV. has been chosen for comparison with the table of Renny, because the true difference of altitude in the two cases is nearly the same. When the tables are laid side by side, the first fact noticed is that the corrections for Switzerland are almost universally smaller numerically, whether positive or negative, than they are for California. This fact is evidently due in part to the use by Renny of a formula containing a special vapor correction, the effect of which is, as has been shown in Chapter I., to reduce the discrepancy between summer and winter measurements. But much more is doubtless due to climatic differences, and this table is heartily welcomed as a strong piece of evidence in confirmation of the view held, even before the investigation in California was begun, that, in order to attain to the best results the world over, it will be necessary to have similar tables prepared for each mountain region, especially if the peculiarities of climate are so marked as they are on the Pacific coast of the United States.

Setting aside the numerical values of the corrections, the general features of the two tables are wonderfully alike. There is a regular gradation in both cases, from morning to midday and thence to evening; though the turning-point in California is from one to two hours later than in Switzerland. If the corrections for the separate hours through the several months are compared with each other along the horizontal lines of the tables, a similar diminution in value from January to spring and summer, and a corresponding rise in the latter part of the year, are observed. The minimum values, however, do not occur in the same months in both cases, particularly for the early morning and late evening hours. The higher latitude of Geneva, and the consequent difference in the times of sunrise and sunset, may possibly have some influence in this respect.

When the separate columns are compared in order to see at what hours a change in the sign of the correction occurs, the coincidence is not absolute, but closer than might be expected. In neither table is there a negative correction for January or December. From February to June the afternoon change from minus to plus takes place, either at the same hour or at points only one hour apart in the two tables. For the forenoons the positive sign prevails in California to a later hour as a rule, but with numerically small values. The hours which give the closest approximation to the truth in the several months agree for some seasons but differ for others, which is not at all surprising, when the local peculiarities of the two countries are taken into account.

In a second table Renny entered side by side with the horary corrections the half-sum of the temperatures observed at the extreme stations, and thus showed that the connections between the greatest errors, whether in excess or defect, and the maximum or minimum of temperature was not so uniform as had been supposed, particularly for the night hours; during the day there was seldom more than one hour's difference between the two critical points.

In applying his table of corrections to the observations of the year

1855, Renny was disappointed at finding that, when he calculated the difference of altitude between Geneva and St. Bernard for those hours in each month at which the horary correction in his table was zero, he obtained results which did not agree exactly with the truth. That this should be so is evident, when it is recollected that mean results derived from observations running through a period of ten or more years would naturally differ in some respects from similar results based upon a shorter period. The practical conclusion drawn by Renny from this apparent failure of his cherished table was " that, although the Table of Horary Corrections meet not our wishes, nor even our expectations, it diminishes (by one half) the errors of the other formulæ. Therefore let us not despond, — all we desire has not been realized, but considerable improvement has been made, and by diligence and zeal more may hereafter be done."

A portion of his concluding remarks presents with so much force the argument for the prosecution of work of this kind, and expresses so exactly the belief which prompted and sustained the investigation in California, that space is taken for an additional quotation. After speaking of the possible future improvements in the constants of the formula, he says : " Small indeed will be such improvements compared to those which will result from the employment of correct tables of horary correction, or from a more correct method than the present one of estimating the mean temperature of the atmospheric column between the stations of barometric observations. To these particular objects all attention ought now to be directed, for here at present is the weak side of barometric levelling. To obtain these objects, too many hands cannot be employed in making observations, ... the results of which, being compared with heights accurately determined by spirit-levelling, may furnish data for such purpose. . . . . But we are warned by the facts of this paper, that with even the assistance of a sound table of local horary corrections, we are not to expect exemption from serious error on all occasions."

The brothers Schlagintweit, while engaged in the service of the East India Company, from the year 1854 to 1858, made a praiseworthy attempt to apply systematic corrections for the daily and yearly variation to their barometric measurements ; but the observations upon which they had to rely were too few in number to establish the values of the corrections beyond question. From their account it appears that the monthly means of observations at four corresponding pairs of stations were computed as a basis for the annual variation, the true difference of altitude being supposed to be known, either by the trigonometrical method, or from the mean of a year's observations with the barometer.*

The annual variation in India does not follow so simple a law as it does in California. In each one of the four cases the existence of two maxima and two minima instead of one was quite clearly indicated; an explanation for which was sought in certain peculiar climatic conditions prevailing at the months of transition from the wet to the dry, or from the dry to the wet season. It seems reasonable, however, to doubt the adequacy of the explanation, and, in view of the anomalies exposed to view in the investigation in California, to hold to the belief that if more extensive series of observations could have been obtained in India, the variation from month to month would have been much more uniform.

The corrections for the hour of the day were computed independently, and were understood to be the quantities by which the results of computation were to be increased or diminished in order to make them agree, not with the annual or corrected mean, but with the monthly mean. To obtain the final result there was still to be added or subtracted the correction for the particular month in question. The observations from which the daily variation was deduced seem not to have been continued for any great length of time at any one place, it being perhaps thought that the amount of change from hour to hour would be the same whatever the season of the year.

In their table of periodic corrections the Messrs. Schlagintweit have also recognized the fact that the corrections per hundred or per thousand feet are greater when the differences of altitude are small than when they are large, and have given three series, calculated for differences of 400, 1,000, and 1,600 feet respectively. For greater altitudes the relative correction was considered the same as for 1,600 feet. Whether this is strictly the case or not, it is evident that the hypsometric results obtained by these explorers in India are entitled to more than a common measure of confi-

---

* Results of a Scientific Mission to India and High Asia. Leipzig and London, 1862, Vol. II. pp. 47 – 64.

dence. The observations were doubtless taken with care, the use of a plumb-line even being recommended in order to secure the verticality of the barometer, and to the computations there was certainly applied every known correction by which a closer approximation to the truth would be reached.

The division of the periodic correction into two parts, one for the month and one for the hour of the day, seems to be an unnecessary, if not a false step. The California tables cannot, indeed, be cited in proof either of this or the contrary statement with much effect, because of the lack of hourly observations, and, for the present, the question will have to be left unsettled.

The subject of the daily period in barometric measurements has also been investigated in minute detail by Professor Bauernfeind of Munich. In August, 1857, with the assistance of eleven students, he determined by spirit-level the height of the top of the Grosser Miesing and of three intermediate stations above the plain. The difference of level between the extreme stations was about 3,650 feet. Half-hourly observations of the barometer, thermometer, psychrometer, and the direction of the wind, were taken, with some omissions, from eight in the morning to six in the evening, between the twentieth and twenty-eighth of the same month. These observations were subjected to a thorough analysis in all respects, and the results published in 1862. The portion relating to the accuracy of the measurements is all that will be referred to at this time.*

The computed differences of altitude when arranged in a tabular form showed " in a surprising manner " that the results were too high between ten o'clock in the morning and four in the afternoon, but too low at earlier or later hours. The obvious relation existing between the computed heights and the daily increase and decrease of the observed temperatures was the first subject for examination. There being no reason to distrust the correctness of the formulæ employed in the computation, the source of error had to be looked for in the observations themselves. If these observations gave the mean temperature correctly, there was no reason why the formula should not give the difference of altitude cor-

---

* Beobachtungen und Untersuchungen über die Genauigkeit barometrischer Höhenmessungen, etc., München, 1862, pp. 59 – 84.

rectly; consequently the conclusion was reached by Bauernfeind, as by so many others, that the stratum of air nearest the surface of the earth is so affected by radiation that the thermometers at the extreme stations do not give the true mean temperature except at certain hours of the day. These hours, according to his observations, are ten in the morning and four in the afternoon. For other hours of the day the observations for temperature are wrong and must be corrected. This view of the subject is essentially the same as that taken by Plantamour; but a different method of obtaining the value of the correction was chosen.

Bauernfeind represented the deviation of the computed from the true height by a formula of the same general character as that used by Kaemtz * in his investigations at the Righi and Faulhorn, and then substituted in place of this formula, for the sake of simplicity in the numerical work, the equations of two common parabolas, one of which coincided almost exactly with that part of the actual curve which represented the changes in the forenoon, and the other with the remainder. With the aid of these equations he computed a table of corrections in degrees to be applied to the observed temperatures in order to get the real mean temperature of the air-column between the two barometers at different hours of the day from eight o'clock until six. No attempt was made to extend the discussion over the hours of the night on account of the lack of observations.

A recomputation of the differences of altitude with the corrected temperatures failed to give absolutely correct results in all cases, but the amount of error was slight and its periodicity disappeared entirely, the variations being fairly chargeable to unavoidable errors of observation.

The inapplicability of his table of corrections for other localities was clearly recognized by Bauernfeind, for he says that, as soon as the temperature correction which he determined for a particular place and season could be extended by long-continued observations over other months and other regions, "we shall be able to make barometric measurements at every hour from morning to evening with almost the same degree of accuracy as we can now at ten in the morning and four in the afternoon." It does not appear from anything published in this connection that

* See page 59.

Bauernfeind's attention had been called to the annual variation, or the effects of the different seasons of the year, any further than to raise a suspicion that the numerical values of the corrections would vary from month to month, without any change in the hours at which the correction is zero.

Having treated of the effects of radiation upon the temperature of the stratum of air in contact with the earth, he next undertook the discussion of the absolute and relative effects of other possible errors of observation, such as the incorrect reading of the attached thermometer, or of the true height of the mercury in the barometer at either station. This discussion was searching and valuable in itself, but developed no new explanation for the observed variations. In fact, it may be said to have strengthened the view that, provided the temperature term can be determined with accuracy, the other incidental errors are of comparatively little importance when the instruments are in good order and the observations are properly made.

It was the daily period, again, which Dr. Rühlmann, while yet a student at Dresden, in 1864, undertook to investigate. He was acquainted with Bauernfeind's work, and hoped to contribute something additional by his own labors. The point selected by him for his observations was the Valtenberg, near Bischofswerda in Saxony, the height of which he determined by spirit-level to be 869 feet. His observations were continued for about six weeks in the months of August and September, 1864, and yielded such results that he was induced to enter upon a critical examination of the records of the meteorological stations of Geneva and St. Bernard, so far as they were accessible to him. The observations of which he made the principal use were those of the six years from 1860 to 1866. This examination carried him considerably beyond the limits originally proposed, and his published book treats largely of the history of the barometer and its use in practical meteorology by aiding in the solution of problems relating to the physics of the atmosphere.*

Rühlmann's summary of the results of his study of the errors to which

---

* Die barometrischen Höhenmessungen, Leipzig, 1870. The opportunity is here taken to acknowledge the debt of thanks which is due to Dr. Rühlmann, particularly for the valuable list of titles of books and memoirs relating to the barometer and its applications. Without this aid the labor of preparing the present chapter would have been increased many fold.

the barometric method of measuring altitudes is liable is comprised in four paragraphs, as follows : —

" I. Heights computed from barometric and thermometric observations are in general essentially greater by day than by night; they show a decided daily period.

" II. Heights computed from daily and monthly means of meteorological observations show a yearly period. They are too small in winter and too great in summer. The amplitude of the yearly period, however, is less than that of the daily.

" III. Yearly means of meteorological observations give heights which differ but little from the true values.

" IV. The periodicity of barometric measurements, both the daily and the yearly, is made up of two parts, one of which, by far the larger, arises from variations in temperature, and the other, the smaller, from variations in the barometer. These two parts have, in general, opposite signs."

The establishment of these four propositions and the discussion of their causes were the principal features of the problem as undertaken by Rühlmann. For the cause of both the daily and the yearly periodicity he looked particularly to the temperature term, after having become satisfied that there were no sources of error in the other parts of the formula which could account for discrepancies so great in amount. The conclusions reached were that the half-sum of the temperatures at the extreme stations does not give the real mean temperature of the column of air, and, as a necessary consequence of this, that the true temperature of the air-column changes, during any given period of time, neither so much nor so rapidly as the arithmetical mean of the temperatures observed at the upper and lower stations. By reversing the computations and considering, as Plantamour did, the true temperature to be the unknown quantity, he obtained mean values of the temperature for every two hours in the month of July; this month being selected because it was the oı which showed the greatest amplitude in the daily period. The results showed that while between four in the morning and two in the afternoon there was, on the average, a variation of 16°.5 F. at Geneva, and of 11° F. at St. Bernard, the variation in the true temperature of the air-column amounted to only 4°.5 F., the minimum occurring at six in the morning and the maximum at six in the evening. Similar computations for the other months led to similar, though numerically smaller results. In December, for instance, the range was 5°.2 at Geneva, and 3°.2 at St. Bernard, but only 1°.3 F. for the true temperature of the air between the two stations.

When the monthly means of recorded temperatures were compared in a similar way with the true mean temperatures of the air-column in the several months, it was found that the range from summer to winter at Geneva amounted to 32°.8 F., and at St. Bernard to 28°.2 F., although the range of the true mean was only 24.°6 F. From such results as these it was evident that the mass of air included between two stations does not become heated so much nor so rapidly as is indicated by thermometers near the earth's surface; that the mass of air shares to only a slight degree the daily variations at the surface; and that it changes in temperature from month to month as a whole at a considerably less rapid rate than do the strata in contact with the surface. The conclusion is therefore inevitable that " the thermometers at the meteorological stations do not give the true temperature of the intervening air-column, but some other quantity," which stands in no simple relation to the true temperature.

One of the practical results of Rühlmann's labors for hypsometrical purposes is the following statement of the hours of the day at which the best approximation to the true differences of height will be attained : —

In January	. . . .	12 M.
" February .	. . . . . .	10 A. M. and 4 P. M.
" March .	. . . . . .	8 " " 6 "
" April	. . . .	7 " " 7 "
" May .	. . . .	7 " " 7 "
" June	. . . . . .	6 " " 9 "
" July .	. . . .	6 " " 9 "
" August .	. . . . . .	7 " " 8 "
" September .	. . . . . .	8 " " 6 "
" October .	. . . . . .	10 " " 4 "
" November .	. . . . . .	11 " " 2 "
" December	. . . .	1 "

No table of corrections to be applied to observations taken at different hours is given; and thus the work of Rühlmann, valuable as it is in all respects, falls short of reaching the point of practical applicability which

was aimed at in the California investigation. The method proposed by
him for finding the true mean temperature of the air between two stations
is too complicated for ordinary use, and requires more labor than the
improved degree of accuracy obtained would justify.

From the foregoing *résumé* it is evident that the existence of a double
periodicity in barometric measurements has attracted the attention of observers for nearly three quarters of a century, but that in almost no instance
has any one pursued the subject far enough to be able to state, with much
approach to accuracy, the probable error of measurements made under
different circumstances. It is to this failure to reach practical results
that the comparative obscurity into which these investigations appear to
have fallen must be ascribed. One of the most striking facts noticed in
the history of this subject is that, almost without exception, each new
investigator entered upon what he thought an untrodden field, entirely
ignorant of the labors of his predecessors, and sought by independent and
original work to remedy or account for difficulties which had arisen in
his own experience.

A long step is taken when the months and hours can be given at
which the errors may be expected to be least; and when the determination of the altitudes of a few prominent points only is undertaken, it
may well be advisable to select the most favorable time for the observations. But upon extensive surveys, when a large tract of country has to
be examined in a short time, and barometric observations have to be
taken at several points in the course of a single day, it becomes necessary
to take at least one step additional. What that step shall be may still
be thought by some an open question; but the choice will have to lie
between a change of the observed reading of the instruments at the two
corresponding stations, and the application of a correction to the computed results. The latter course, which recommends itself by its greater
simplicity and equal accuracy, is the one which seems most likely to give
good results for California and the Pacific coast.

TABLES.

I.

SACRAMENTO AND COLFAX. (First Year.)

By Railroad Survey, 2399 feet.

Date.	7 A. M.		2 P. M.		9 P. M.		Mean.	
1870 October	2357.9	—41.1	2457.4	+58.4	2370.0	—29.0	2393.4	— 5.6
November	2353.9	—45.1	2435.6	+36.6	2368.6	—30.4	2386.5	—12.5
December	2357.8	—41.2	2435.2	+36.2	2374.5	—24.5	2389.5	— 9.5
1871 January	2353.0	—46.0	2425.3	+26.3	2362.7	—36.3	2380.2	—18.8
February	2372.1	—26.9	2432.4	+33.4	2405.5	+ 6.5	2402.8	+ 3.8
March	2388.3	—10.7	2455.2	+56.2	2395.8	— 3.2	2412.9	+13.9
April	2385.8	—13.2	2459.9	+60.9	2387.4	—11.6	2410.6	+11.6
May	2419.1	+20.1	2477.8	+78.8	2411.6	+12.6	2435.6	+36.6
June	2410.8	+11.8	2493.6	+94.6	2386.7	—12.3	2430.3	+31.3
July	2416.9	+17.9	2490.1	+91.1	2399.1	+ 0.1	2435.5	+36.5
August	2402.8	+ 3.8	2490.7	+91.7	2379.5	—19.5	2424.9	+25.9
September	2377.9	—21.1	2479.5	+80.5	2371.9	—27.1	2409.6	+10.6
Mean of Year	2383.0	—16.0	2461.1	+62.1	2384.4	—14.6	2409.3	+10.3

II.

SACRAMENTO AND COLFAX. (Second Year.)

By Railroad Survey, 2399 feet.

Date.	7 A. M.		2 P. M.		9 P. M.		Mean.	
1871 October	2360.6	—38.4	2471.4	+72.4	2365.5	—33.5	2398.9	— 0.1
November	2360.5	—38.5	2439.3	+40.3	2371.8	—27.2	2389.9	— 9.1
December	2379.1	—19.9	2421.1	+22.1	2404.9	+ 5.9	2400.9	+ 1.9
1872 January	2371.8	—27.2	2425.1	+26.1	2388.9	—10.1	2395.4	— 3.6
February	2383.4	—15.6	2421.2	+22.2	2387.9	—11.1	2397.5	— 1.5
March	2402.0	+ 3.0	2443.8	+44.8	2391.0	— 8.0	2412.4	+13.4
April	2426.5	+27.5	2453.8	+54.8	2406.6	+ 7.6	2429.2	+30.2
May	2432.4	+33.4	2463.7	+64.7	2395.5	— 3.5	2431.1	+32.1
June	2421.6	+22.6	2441.8	+42.8	2386.7	—12.3	2416.5	+17.5
July	2441.2	+42.2	2481.0	+82.0	2397.8	— 1.2	2440.6	+41.6
August	2407.1	+ 8.1	2466.1	+67.1	2372.7	—26.3	2415.1	+16.1
September	2370.7	—28.3	2433.1	+34.1	2366.2	—32.8	2389.3	— 9.7
Mean of Year	2396.4	— 2.6	2446.8	+47.8	2386.3	—12.7	2409.7	+10.7

III.

SACRAMENTO AND COLFAX. (Third Year.)

By Railroad Survey, 2399 feet.

Date.	7 A. M.		2 P. M.		9 P. M.		Mean.	
1872 October	2353.4	—45.6	2429.0	+ 30.0	2336.4	—62.6	2372.9	—26.1
November	2380.2	—18.8	2433.6	+ 34.6	2360.9	—38.1	2392.1	— 6.9
December	2354.2	—44.8	2424.3	+ 25.3	2364.1	—34.9	2381.2	—17.8
1873 January	2362.3	—36.7	2445.5	+ 46.5	2372.7	—26.3	2393.3	— 5.7
February	2385.1	—13.9	2430.2	+ 31.2	2392.3	— 6.7	2402.8	+ 3.8
March	2389.7	— 9.3	2470.8	+ 71.8	2390.5	— 8.5	2417.3	+18.3
April	2448.0	+49.0	2512.1	+113.1	2458.9	+59.9	2472.8	+73.8
May	2447.3	+48.3	2494.9	+ 95.9	2422.8	+23.8	2454.4	+55.4
June	2457.7	+58.7	2535.6	+136.6	2432.0	+33.0	2474.7	+75.7
July	2445.6	+46.6	2482.3	+ 83.3	2426.4	+27.4	2451.2	+52.2
August	2459.3	+60.3	2516.9	+117.9	2430.1	+31.1	2469.5	+70.5
September	2382.5	—16.5	2462.4	+ 63.4	2388.9	—10.1	2410.7	+11.7
Mean of Year	2405.4	+ 6.4	2469.8	+ 70.8	2398.0	— 1.0	2424.4	+25.4

IV.

SACRAMENTO AND SUMMIT. (First Year.)

By Railroad Survey, 6989 feet.

Date.	7 A. M.		2 P. M.		9 P. M.		Mean.	
1870 October	6778.4	—210.6	7037.7	+ 48.7	6819.6	—169.4	6879.8	—109.2
November	6760.5	—228.5	7006.9	+ 17.9	6817.5	—171.5	6862.2	—126.8
December	6750.7	—238.3	6963.5	— 25.5	6817.9	—171.1	6844.5	—144.5
1871 January	6776.8	—212.2	6961.1	— 27.9	6823.4	—165.6	6853.9	—135.1
February	6851.7	—137.3	7040.1	+ 51.1	6920.6	— 68.4	6936.5	— 52.5
March	6887.4	—101.6	7080.7	+ 91.7	6915.4	— 73.6	6961.1	— 27.9
April	6924.6	— 64.4	7112.6	+123.6	6894.4	— 94.6	6976.6	— 12.4
May	6972.7	— 16.3	7134.3	+145.3	6921.3	— 67.7	7008.8	+ 19.8
June	6946.1	— 42.9	7160.1	+171.1	6891.4	— 97.6	6998.4	+ 9.4
July	6881.5	—107.5	7135.2	+146.2	6876.0	—113.0	6965.1	— 23.9
August	6839.5	—149.5	7154.2	+165.2	6825.1	—163.9	6940.2	— 48.8
September	6856.9	—132.1	7115.1	+126.1	6836.6	—152.4	6936.8	— 52.2
Mean of Year	6852.2	—136.8	7075.1	+ 86.1	6863.3	—125.7	6930.3	— 58.7

V.

SACRAMENTO AND SUMMIT. (Second Year.)

By Railroad Survey, 6989 feet.

Date.	7 A. M.		2 P. M.		9 P. M.		Mean.	
1871 October	6771.9	—217.1	7100.7	+111.7	6810.7	—178.3	6894.2	—94.8
November	6825.8	—163.2	7051.4	+ 62.4	6869.5	—119.5	6915.2	—73.8
December	6868.8	—120.2	6989.6	+ 0.6	6912.7	— 76.3	6923.0	—66.0
1872 January	6848.5	—140.5	6964.6	— 24.4	6893.1	— 95.9	6902.2	—86.8
February	6959.2	— 29.8	7020.1	+ 31.1	6978.3	— 10.7	6985.8	— 3.2
March	6929.2	— 59.8	7033.5	+ 44.5	6951.5	— 37.5	6970.8	—18.2
April	6968.1	— 20.9	7065.4	+ 76.4	6961.0	— 28.0	6998.5	+ 9.5
May	6936.3	— 52.7	7064.9	+ 75.9	6904.1	— 84.9	6968.3	—20.7
June	6950.9	— 38.1	7076.0	+ 87.0	6886.5	—102.5	6970.9	—18.1
July	6934.9	— 54.1	7096.0	+107.0	6887.7	—101.3	6973.1	—15.9
August	6883.2	—105.8	7097.3	+108.3	6879.9	—109.1	6953.2	—35.8
September	6848.4	—140.6	7073.9	+ 84.9	6887.3	—101.7	6936.4	—52.6
Mean of Year	6893.8	— 95.2	7052.8	+ 63.8	6901.9	— 87.1	6949.3	—39.7

VI.

SACRAMENTO AND SUMMIT. (Third Year.)

By Railroad Survey, 6989 feet.

Date.	7 A. M.		2 P. M.		9 P. M.		Mean.	
1872 October	6814.2	—174.8	7070.0	+ 81.0	6858.5	—130.5	6914.7	— 74.3
November	6809.5	—179.5	7030.3	+ 41.3	6829.9	—159.1	6889.8	— 99.2
December	6799.1	—189.9	6976.5	— 12.5	6839.7	—149.3	6871.5	—117.5
1873 January	6844.9	—144.1	7015.7	+ 26.7	6884.5	—104.5	6914.4	— 74.6
February	6961.6	— 27.4	7089.6	+100.6	6989.4	+ 0.4	7013.3	+ 24.3
March	6881.4	—107.6	7083.5	+ 94.5	6925.2	— 63.8	6963.3	— 25.7
April	7002.8	+ 13.8	7150.6	+161.6	7012.4	+ 23.4	7055.7	+ 66.7
May	6977.7	— 11.3	7181.3	+192.3	6970.6	— 18.4	7042.8	+ 53.8
June	6969.2	— 19.8	7173.8	+184.8	6985.7	— 3.3	7041.9	+ 52.9
July	6957.2	— 31.8	7088.3	+ 99.3	6983.3	— 5.7	7010.3	+ 21.3
August	6999.0	+ 10.0	7161.7	+172.7	7015.0	+ 26.0	7059.4	+ 70.4
* September	6852.6	—136.4	7094.5	+105.5	6861.9	—127.1	6936.6	— 52.4
Mean of Year	6905.8	— 83.2	7093.0	+104.0	6929.7	— 59.3	6976.1	— 12.9

* Mean of First and Second Years.

VII.

COLFAX AND SUMMIT. (First Year.)

By Railroad Survey, 4590 feet.

Date.	7 A. M.		2 P. M.		9 P. M.		Mean.	
1870 October	4475.4	—114.6	4630.7	+ 40.7	4493.9	— 96.1	4534.7	—55.3
November	4471.3	—118.7	4614.3	+ 24.3	4496.9	— 93.1	4526.9	—63.1
December	4453.9	—136.1	4584.0	— 6.0	4488.9	—101.1	4509.4	—80.6
1871 January	4483.7	—106.3	4606.3	+ 16.3	4512.1	— 77.9	4534.1	—55.9
February	4517.4	— 72.6	4638.0	+ 48.0	4538.4	— 51.6	4564.3	—25.7
March	4541.1	— 48.9	4650.3	+ 60.3	4543.5	— 46.5	4578.1	—11.9
April	4582.3	— 7.7	4684.3	+ 94.3	4533.3	— 56.7	4599.8	+ 9.8
May	4597.4	+ 7.4	4690.3	+100.3	4535.6	— 54.4	4608.3	+18.3
June	4604.0	+ 14.0	4719.3	+129.3	4555.6	— 34.4	4626.7	+36.7
July	4563.4	— 26.6	4719.6	+129.6	4552.6	— 37.4	4612.3	+22.3
August	4540.8	— 49.2	4728.7	+138.7	4526.3	— 63.7	4598.4	+ 8.4
September	4530.8	— 59.2	4697.3	+107.3	4512.0	— 78.0	4581.1	— 8.9
Mean of Year	4530.1	— 59.9	4663.6	+ 73.6	4524.1	— 65.9	4572.8	—17.2

VIII.

COLFAX AND SUMMIT. (Second Year.)

By Railroad Survey, 4590 feet.

Date.	7 A. M.		2 P. M.		9 P. M.		Mean.	
1871 October	4481.9	—108.1	4680.5	+ 90.5	4506.0	—84.0	4556.3	—33.7
November	4520.8	— 69.2	4652.9	+ 62.9	4550.0	—40.0	4575.2	—14.8
December	4543.4	— 46.6	4643.5	+ 53.5	4568.3	—21.7	4584.9	— 5.1
1872 January	4508.4	— 81.6	4621.0	+ 31.0	4537.9	—52.1	4556.0	—34.0
February	4592.6	+ 2.6	4641.1	+ 51.1	4615.3	+25.3	4616.7	+26.7
March	4558.9	— 31.1	4644.7	+ 54.7	4585.4	— 4.6	4596.1	+ 6.1
April	4567.8	— 22.2	4653.8	+ 63.8	4573.5	—16.5	4598.0	+ 8.0
May	4561.6	— 28.4	4668.7	+ 78.7	4565.2	—24.8	4597.9	+ 7.9
June	4578.1	— 11.9	4709.2	+119.2	4564.8	—25.2	4617.7	+27.7
July	4567.8	— 22.2	4703.4	+113.4	4567.5	—22.5	4613.4	+23.4
August	4548.4	— 41.6	4729.0	+139.0	4544.1	—45.9	4606.6	+16.6
September	4538.8	— 51.2	4705.4	+115.4	4556.6	—33.4	4599.8	+ 9.8
Mean of Year	4547.4	— 42.6	4671.1	+ 81.1	4561.2	—28.8	4593.2	+ 3.2

IX.

COLFAX AND SUMMIT. (Third Year.)

By Railroad Survey, 4590 feet.

Date.	7 A. M.		2 P. M.		9 P. M.		Mean.	
1872 October	4522.5	— 67.5	4701.9	+111.9	4566.2	—23.8	4597.6	+ 7.6
November	4488.9	—101.1	4648.8	+ 58.8	4521.8	—68.2	4553.5	—36.5
December	4494.1	— 95.9	4608.6	+ 18.6	4518.5	—71.5	4539.5	—50.5
1873 January	4531.1	— 58.9	4624.0	+ 34.0	4555.8	—34.2	4569.9	—20.1
February	4583.2	— 6.8	4667.2	+ 77.2	4592.8	+ 2.8	4613.5	+23.5
March	4532.0	— 58.0	4658.9	+ 68.9	4555.7	—34.3	4581.7	— 8.3
April	4558.2	— 31.8	4662.5	+ 72.5	4571.8	—18.2	4598.1	+ 8.1
May	4562.2	— 27.8	4724.8	+134.8	4572.2	—17.8	4619.6	+29.6
June	4562.5	— 27.5	4710.8	+120.8	4582.7	— 7.3	4618.3	+28.3
July	4573.7	— 16.3	4695.8	+105.8	4585.2	— 4.8	4618.2	+28.2
August	4615.2	+ 25.2	4744.1	+154.1	4643.2	+53.2	4667.7	+77.7
* September	4534.8	— 55.2	4701.3	+111.3	4534.3	—55.7	4590.5	+ 0.5
Mean of Year	4546.5	— 43.5	4679.1	+ 89.1	4566.7	—23.3	4597.3	+ 7.3

* Mean of First and Second Years.

X.

SACRAMENTO AND COLFAX. (Mean of Three Years.)

By Railroad Survey, 2399 feet.

Month.	7 A. M.		2 P. M.		9 P. M.		Mean.	
October	2357.3	—41.7	2452.6	+53.6	2357.3	—41.7	2388.4	—10.6
November	2364.9	—34.1	2436.2	+37.2	2367.1	—31.9	2389.5	— 9.5
December	2363.7	—35.3	2426.9	+27.9	2381.2	—17.8	2390.5	— 8.5
January	2362.4	—36.6	2432.0	+33.0	2374.8	—24.2	2389.6	— 9.4
February	2380.2	—18.8	2427.9	+28.9	2395.2	— 3.8	2401.0	+ 2.0
March	2393.3	— 5.7	2456.6	+57.6	2392.4	— 6.6	2414.2	+15.2
April	2420.1	+21.1	2475.3	+76.3	2417.6	+18.6	2437.5	+38.5
May	2432.9	+33.9	2478.8	+79.8	2410.0	+11.0	2440.4	+41.4
June	2430.0	+31.0	2490.3	+91.3	2401.8	+ 2.8	2440.5	+41.5
July	2434.6	+35.6	2484.5	+85.5	2407.8	+ 8.8	2442.4	+43.4
August	2423.1	+24.1	2491.2	+92.2	2394.1	— 4.9	2436.5	+37.5
September	2377.0	—22.0	2458.3	+59.3	2375.7	—23.3	2403.2	+ 4.2
Mean	2394.9	— 4.1	2459.2	+60.2	2389.6	— 9.4	2414.5	+15.5

XI.

SACRAMENTO AND SUMMIT. (Mean of Three Years.)

By Railroad Survey, 6989 feet.

Month.	7 A. M.		2 P. M.		9 P. M.		Mean.	
October	6788.2	—200.8	7069.5	+ 80.5	6829.6	—159.4	6896.2	— 92.8
November	6798.6	—190.4	7029.5	+ 40.5	6839.0	—150.0	6889.1	— 99.9
December	6806.2	—182.8	6976.5	— 12.5	6856.8	—132.2	6879.7	—109.3
January	6823.4	—165.6	6980.5	— 8.5	6867.0	—122.0	6890.2	—108.8
February	6924.2	— 64.8	7049.9	+ 60.9	6962.8	— 26.2	6978.5	— 20.5
March	6899.3	— 89.7	7065.9	+ 76.9	6930.7	— 58.3	6965.1	— 23.9
April	6965.2	— 23.8	7109.5	+120.5	6955.9	— 33.1	7010.3	+ 21.3
May	6962.2	— 26.8	7126.8	+137.8	6932.0	— 57.0	7006.6	+ 17.6
June	6955.4	— 33.6	7136.6	+147.6	6921.2	— 67.8	7003.7	+ 14.7
July	6924.5	— 64.5	7106.5	+117.5	6915.7	— 73.3	6982.8	— 6.2
August	6907.2	— 81.8	7137.7	+148.7	6906.7	— 82.3	6984.3	— 4.7
September	6852.6	—136.4	7094.5	+105.5	6861.9	—127.1	6936.6	— 52.4
Mean	6883.9	—105.1	7073.6	+ 84.6	6898.3	— 90.7	6951.9	— 37.1

XII.

COLFAX AND SUMMIT. (Mean of Three Years.)

By Railroad Survey, 4590 feet.

Month.	7 A. M.		2 P. M.		9 P. M.		Mean.	
October	4493.2	—96.8	4671.0	+ 81.0	4522.0	—68.0	4562.9	—27.1
November	4493.7	—96.3	4638.7	+ 48.7	4522.9	—67.1	4551.9	—38.1
December	4497.1	—92.9	4612.0	+ 22.0	4525.2	—64.8	4544.6	—45.4
January	4507.7	—82.3	4617.1	+ 27.1	4535.3	—54.7	4553.3	—36.7
February	4564.4	—25.6	4648.8	+ 58.8	4582.2	— 7.8	4598.2	+ 8.2
March	4544.0	—46.0	4651.3	+ 61.3	4561.5	—28.5	4585.3	— 4.7
April	4569.4	—20.6	4666.9	+ 76.9	4559.5	—30.5	4598.6	+ 8.6
May	4573.7	—16.3	4694.6	+104.6	4557.7	—32.3	4608.6	+18.6
June	4581.5	— 8.5	4713.1	+123.1	4567.7	—22.3	4620.9	+30.9
July	4568.3	—21.7	4706.3	+116.3	4568.4	—21.6	4614.6	+24.6
August	4568.1	—21.9	4733.9	+143.9	4571.2	—18.8	4624.2	+34.2
September	4534.8	—55.2	4701.3	+111.3	4534.3	—55.7	4590.5	+ 0.5
Mean	4541.3	—48.7	4671.3	+ 81.3	4550.7	—39.3	4587.8	— 2.2

XIII.

SACRAMENTO AND SUMMIT. (First Year.)

Date.	VARIATION FROM RAILROAD SURVEY.								DIFFERENCES.			
	Direct.				With intermediate Station.							
	7 A. M.	2 P. M.	9 P. M.	Mean of Day.	7 A. M.	2 P. M.	9 P. M.	Mean of Day.	7 A. M.	2 P.M.	9 P.M.	Mean of Day.
1870 Oct.	—210.6	+ 48.7	—169.4	—109.2	—155.7	+ 99.1	—125.1	— 60.9	54.9	50.4	44.3	48.3
Nov.	—228.5	+ 17.9	—171.5	—126.8	—163.8	+ 60.9	—123.5	— 75.6	64.7	43.0	48.0	51.2
Dec.	—238.3	— 25.5	—171.1	—144.5	—177.3	+ 30.2	—125.6	— 90.1	61.0	55.7	45.5	54.4
1871 Jan.	—212.2	— 27.9	—165.6	—135.1	—152.3	+ 42.6	—114.2	— 74.7	59.9	70.5	51.4	60.4
Feb.	—137.3	+ 51.1	— 68.4	— 52.5	— 99.5	+ 81.4	— 45.1	— 21.9	37.8	30.3	23.3	30.6
Mar.	—101.6	+ 91.7	— 73.6	— 27.9	— 59.6	+116.5	— 49.7	+ 2.0	42.0	24.8	23.9	29.9
Apr.	— 64.4	+123.6	— 94.6	— 12.4	— 20.9	+155.2	— 68.3	+21.4	43.5	31.6	26.3	33.8
May	— 16.3	+145.3	— 67.7	+ 19.8	+ 27.5	+179.1	— 41.8	+54.9	43.8	33.8	25.9	35.1
June	— 42.9	+171.1	— 97.6	+ 9.4	+ 25.8	+223.9	— 46.7	+68.0	68.7	52.8	50.9	58.6
July	—107.5	+146.2	—113.0	— 23.9	— 8.7	+220.7	— 37.3	+58.8	98.8	74.5	75.7	82.7
Aug.	—149.5	+165.2	—163.9	— 48.8	— 45.4	+230.4	— 83.2	+34.3	104.1	65.2	80.7	83.1
Sept.	—132.1	+126.1	—152.4	— 52.2	— 80.3	+187.8	—105.1	+ 1.7	51.8	61.7	47.3	53.9
Mean	—136.8	+ 86.1	—125.7	— 58.7	— 75.9	+135.7	— 80.5	— 6.8	60.9	49.5	45.3	51.8

XIV.

SACRAMENTO AND SUMMIT. (Second Year.)

Date.	VARIATION FROM RAILROAD SURVEY.								DIFFERENCES.			
	Direct.				With intermediate Station.							
	7 A. M.	2 P. M.	9 P. M.	Mean of Day.	7 A. M.	2 P. M.	9 P. M.	Mean of Day.	7 A. M.	2 P.M.	9 P.M.	Mean of Day.
1871 Oct.	—217.1	+111.7	—178.3	— 94.8	—146.5	+162.9	—117.5	— 33.8	70.6	51.2	60.8	61.0
Nov.	—163.2	+ 62.4	—119.5	— 73.8	—107.7	+103.2	— 67.2	— 23.9	55.5	40.8	52.3	49.9
Dec.	—120.2	+ 0.6	— 76.3	— 66.0	— 66.5	+ 75.6	— 15.8	— 3.2	53.7	75.0	60.5	62.8
1872 Jan.	—140.5	— 24.4	— 95.9	— 86.8	—108.8	+ 57.1	— 62.2	— 37.6	31.7	81.5	33.7	49.2
Feb.	— 29.8	+ 31.1	— 10.7	— 3.2	— 13.0	+ 73.3	+ 14.2	+ 25.2	16.8	42.2	24.9	28.4
Mar.	— 59.8	+ 44.5	— 37.5	— 18.2	— 28.1	+ 99.5	— 12.6	+ 19.5	31.7	55.0	24.9	37.7
Apr.	— 20.9	+ 76.4	— 28.0	+ 9.5	+ 5.3	+118.6	— 8.9	+ 38.2	26.2	42.2	19.1	28.7
May	— 52.7	+ 75.9	— 84.9	— 20.7	+ 5.0	+143.4	— 28.3	+ 40.0	57.7	67.5	56.6	60.7
June	— 38.1	+ 87.0	—102.5	— 18.1	+ 10.7	+162.0	— 37.5	+ 45.2	48.8	75.0	65.0	63.3
July	— 54.1	+107.0	—101.3	— 15.9	+ 18.6	+189.3	— 20.6	+ 63.0	72.7	82.3	80.7	78.9
Aug.	—105.8	+108.3	—109.1	— 35.8	— 34.3	+204.5	— 70.7	+ 33.1	71.5	96.2	38.4	68.9
Sept.	—140.6	+ 84.9	—101.7	— 52.6	— 73.3	+154.6	— 60.5	+ 5.7	67.3	69.7	41.2	58.3
Mean	— 95.2	+ 63.8	— 87.1	— 39.7	— 41.9	+128.7	— 40.6	+ 14.3	50.3	64.9	46.5	54.0

XV.

SACRAMENTO AND SUMMIT. (Third Year.)

Date.	Direct.				With intermediate Station.				Differences.			
	7 A. M.	2 P. M.	9 P. M.	Mean of Day.	7 A. M.	2 P. M.	9 P. M.	Mean of Day.	7 A. M.	2 P.M.	9 P.M.	Mean of Day.
1872 Oct.	−174.8	+ 81.0	−130.5	− 74.3	−113.7	+142.1	− 83.0	− 17.9	61.1	61.1	47.5	56.4
Nov.	−179.5	+ 41.3	−159.1	− 99.5	−120.1	+ 89.7	−108.0	− 46.1	59.4	48.4	51.1	53.1
Dec.	−189.9	− 12.5	−149.3	−117.5	−140.7	+ 43.9	−106.4	− 68.3	49.2	56.4	42.9	49.2
1873 Jan.	−144.1	+ 26.7	−104.5	− 74.6	− 95.6	+ 80.5	− 60.5	− 25.8	48.5	53.8	44.0	48.8
Feb.	− 27.4	+100.6	+ 0.4	+ 24.3	− 20.7	+108.4	− 3.9	+ 27.3	6.7	7.8	−4.3	3.0
Mar.	−107.6	+ 94.5	− 63.8	− 25.7	− 67.3	+140.7	− 42.8	+ 10.0	40.3	46.2	21.0	35.7
Apr.	+ 13.8	+161.6	+ 23.4	+ 66.7	+ 17.2	+185.6	+ 41.7	+ 81.9	3.4	24.0	18.3	15.2
May	− 11.3	+192.3	− 18.4	+ 53.8	+ 20.5	+230.7	+ 6.0	+ 85.0	31.8	38.4	24.4	31.2
June	− 19.8	+184.8	− 3.3	+ 52.9	+ 31.2	+257.4	+ 25.7	+104.0	51.0	72.6	29.0	51.1
July	− 31.8	+ 99.3	− 5.7	+ 21.3	+ 30.3	+189.1	+ 22.6	+ 80.4	62.1	89.8	28.3	59.1
Aug.	+ 10.0	+172.7	+ 26.0	+ 70.4	+ 85.5	+172.0	+ 84.3	+148.2	75.5	−0.7	58.3	77.8
Sept.	−136.4	+105.5	−127.1	− 52.4	− 71.7	+174.7	− 65.8	+ 12.2	64.7	69.2	61.3	64.6
Mean	− 83.2	+104.0	− 59.3	− 12.9	− 37.1	+159.9	− 24.3	+ 32.7	46.1	55.9	35.0	45.6

XVI.

SACRAMENTO AND SUMMIT. (Mean of Three Years.)

Month.	Direct.				With intermediate Station.				Differences.			
	7 A. M.	2 P. M.	9 P. M.	Mean of Day.	7 A. M.	2 P. M.	9 P. M.	Mean of Day.	7 A. M.	2 P.M.	9 P.M.	Mean of Day.
Oct.	−200.8	+ 80.5	−159.4	− 92.8	−138.5	+134.6	−109.7	−37.7	62.3	54.1	49.7	55.1
Nov.	−190.4	+ 40.5	−150.0	− 99.9	−130.4	+ 85.9	− 99.0	−47.6	60.0	45.4	51.0	52.3
Dec.	−182.8	− 12.5	−132.2	−109.3	−128.2	+ 49.9	− 82.6	−53.9	54.6	62.4	49.6	55.4
Jan.	−165.6	− 8.5	−122.0	− 98.8	−118.9	+ 60.1	− 78.9	−46.1	46.7	68.6	43.1	52.7
Feb.	− 64.8	+ 60.9	− 26.2	− 10.5	− 44.4	+ 87.7	− 11.6	+10.2	20.4	26.8	14.6	20.7
Mar.	− 89.7	+ 76.9	− 58.3	− 23.9	− 51.7	+118.9	− 35.1	+10.5	38.0	42.0	23.1	34.4
Apr.	− 23.8	+120.5	− 33.1	+ 21.3	+ 0.5	+153.2	− 11.9	+47.1	24.3	32.7	21.2	25.8
May	− 26.8	+137.8	− 57.0	+ 17.6	+ 17.6	+184.4	− 21.3	+60.0	44.4	46.6	35.7	42.4
June	− 33.6	+147.6	− 67.8	+ 14.7	+ 22.5	+214.4	− 19.5	+72.4	56.1	66.8	48.3	57.7
July	− 64.5	+117.5	− 73.3	− 6.2	+ 13.9	+201.8	− 12.8	+68.0	78.4	84.3	60.5	74.2
Aug.	− 81.8	+148.7	− 82.3	− 4.7	+ 2.2	+236.1	− 23.7	+71.7	84.0	87.4	58.6	76.4
Sept.	−136.4	+105.5	−127.1	− 52.4	− 77.2	+170.6	− 79.0	+ 4.7	59.2	65.1	48.1	57.1
Mean	−105.1	+ 84.6	− 90.7	− 37.1	− 52.7	+141.5	− 48.7	+13.3	52.4	56.9	42.0	50.4

XVII.

SACRAMENTO AND COLFAX.

COMPARISON OF RESULTS FOR THREE YEARS, SHOWING THEIR RANGE AND VARIATIONS FROM RAILROAD SURVEY.

Month	7 A. M.					2 P. M.					9 P. M.					Mean				
	1st Year.	2d Year.	3d Year.	Mean.	Range.	1st Year.	2d Year.	3d Year.	Mean.	Range.	1st Year.	2d Year.	3d Year.	Mean.	Range.	1st Year.	2d Year.	3d Year.	Mean.	Range.
Oct.	—41.1	—38.4	—45.6	—41.7	7.2	+58.4	+72.4	+30.0	+53.6	42.4	—29.0	—33.5	—62.6	—41.7	33.6	— 5.6	— 0.1	—26.1	—10.6	26.0
Nov.	—45.1	—38.5	—18.8	—34.1	26.3	+36.6	+40.3	+34.6	+37.2	5.7	—30.4	—27.2	—38.1	—31.9	10.9	—12.5	— 9.1	— 6.9	— 9.5	5.6
Dec.	—41.2	—19.9	—44.8	—35.3	24.9	+36.2	+22.1	+25.3	+27.9	14.1	—24.5	+ 5.9	—34.9	—17.8	40.8	— 9.5	+ 1.9	—17.8	— 8.5	19.7
Jan.	—46.0	—27.2	—36.7	—36.6	18.8	+26.3	+26.1	+46.5	+33.0	20.4	—36.3	—10.1	—26.3	—24.2	26.2	—18.8	— 3.6	— 5.7	— 9.4	15.2
Feb.	—26.9	—15.6	—13.9	—18.8	13.0	+33.4	+22.2	+31.2	+28.9	11.2	+ 6.5	—11.1	— 6.7	— 3.8	17.6	+ 3.8	— 1.5	+ 3.8	+ 2.0	5.3
Mar.	—10.7	+ 3.0	— 9.3	— 5.7	13.7	+56.2	+44.8	+71.8	+57.6	27.0	— 3.2	— 8.0	— 8.5	— 6.6	5.3	+13.9	+13.4	+18.3	+15.2	4.9
Apr.	—13.2	+27.5	+49.0	+21.1	62.2	+60.9	+54.8	+113.1	+76.3	58.3	—11.6	+ 7.6	+59.9	+18.6	61.5	+11.6	+30.2	+73.8	+38.5	62.2
May	+20.1	+33.4	+48.3	+33.9	28.2	+78.8	+64.7	+95.9	+79.8	31.2	+12.6	+ 3.5	+23.8	+11.0	27.3	+36.6	+32.1	+55.4	+41.4	23.3
June	+11.8	+22.6	+58.7	+31.0	46.9	+94.6	+42.8	+136.6	+91.3	93.8	—12.3	—12.3	+33.0	+ 2.8	45.3	+31.3	+17.5	+75.7	+41.5	58.2
July	+17.9	+42.2	+46.6	+35.6	28.7	+91.1	+82.0	+83.3	+85.5	9.1	+ 0.1	+ 1.2	+27.4	+ 8.8	28.6	+36.5	+41.6	+52.2	+43.4	15.7
Aug.	+ 3.8	+ 8.1	+60.3	+24.1	56.5	+91.7	+67.1	+117.9	+92.2	50.8	—19.5	—26.3	+31.1	— 4.9	57.4	+25.9	+16.1	+70.5	+37.5	54.4
Sept.	—21.1	—28.3	—16.5	—22.0	11.8	+80.5	+34.1	+63.4	+59.3	46.4	—27.1	—32.8	—10.1	—23.3	22.7	+10.6	— 9.7	+11.7	+ 4.2	21.4
Mean	—16.0	— 2.6	+ 6.4	— 4.1	22.4	+62.1	+47.8	+70.8	+60.2	23.0	—14.6	—12.7	— 1.0	— 9.4	13.6	+10.3	+10.7	+25.4	+15.5	15.1

XVIII.

SACRAMENTO AND SUMMIT.

COMPARISON OF RESULTS FOR THREE YEARS, SHOWING THEIR RANGE AND VARIATIONS FROM RAILROAD SURVEY.

Month	7 A. M.					2 P. M.					9 P. M.					Mean.				
	1st Year.	2d Year.	3d Year.	Mean.	Range.	1st Year.	2d Year.	3d Year.	Mean.	Range.	1st Year.	2d Year.	3d Year.	Mean.	Range.	1st Year.	2d Year.	3d Year.	Mean.	Range.
Oct.	−210.6	−217.1	−174.8	−200.8	42.3	+48.7	+111.7	+81.0	+80.5	63.0	−169.4	−178.3	−130.5	−159.4	47.8	−109.2	−94.8	−74.3	−92.8	34.9
Nov.	−228.5	−163.2	−179.5	−190.4	65.3	+17.9	+62.4	+41.3	+40.5	44.5	−171.5	−119.5	−159.1	−150.0	52.0	−126.8	−73.8	−99.2	−99.9	53.0
Dec.	−238.3	−120.2	−189.9	−182.8	118.1	−25.5	+0.6	−12.5	−12.5	26.1	−171.1	−76.3	−149.3	−132.2	94.8	−144.5	−66.0	−117.5	−109.3	78.5
Jan.	−212.2	−140.5	−144.1	−165.6	71.7	−27.9	−24.4	+26.7	−8.5	54.6	−165.6	−95.9	−104.5	−122.0	69.7	−135.1	−86.8	−74.6	−98.8	60.5
Feb.	−137.3	−29.8	−27.4	−64.8	109.9	+51.1	+31.1	+100.6	+60.9	69.5	−68.4	−10.7	+0.4	−26.2	68.8	−52.5	+3.2	+24.3	−10.5	76.8
Mar.	−101.6	−59.8	−107.6	−89.7	47.8	+91.7	+44.5	+94.5	+76.9	50.0	−73.6	−37.5	−63.8	−58.3	36.1	−27.9	−18.2	−25.7	−23.9	9.7
Apr.	−64.4	−20.9	+13.8	−23.8	78.2	+123.6	+76.4	+161.6	+120.5	85.2	−94.6	−28.0	+23.4	−33.1	118.0	−12.4	+9.5	+66.7	+21.3	79.1
May	−16.3	−52.7	−11.3	−26.8	41.4	+145.3	+75.9	+192.3	+137.8	116.4	−67.7	−84.9	−18.4	−57.0	66.5	−19.8	−20.7	+53.8	+17.6	74.5
June	−42.9	−38.1	−19.8	−33.6	23.1	+171.1	+87.0	+184.8	+147.6	97.8	−97.6	−102.5	−3.3	−67.8	99.2	+9.4	+18.1	+52.9	+14.7	71.0
July	−107.5	−54.1	−31.8	−64.5	75.7	+146.2	+107.0	+99.3	+117.5	46.9	−113.0	−101.3	+5.7	−73.3	107.3	−23.9	−15.9	+21.3	−6.2	45.2
Aug.	−149.5	−105.8	+10.0	−81.8	159.5	+165.2	+108.3	+172.7	+148.7	64.4	−163.9	−109.1	+26.0	−82.3	189.9	−48.8	+35.8	+70.4	+4.7	119.2
Sept.	−132.1	−140.6	−136.4	−136.4	8.5	+126.1	+84.9	+105.5	+105.5	41.2	−152.4	−101.7	−127.1	−127.1	50.7	−52.2	−52.6	−52.4	−52.4	0.4
Mean	−136.8	−95.2	−83.2	−105.1	54.6	+86.1	+63.8	+104.0	+84.6	40.2	−125.7	−87.1	−59.3	−90.7	66.4	−58.7	−39.7	−12.9	−37.1	45.8

XIX.

COLFAX AND SUMMIT.

COMPARISON OF RESULTS FOR THREE YEARS, SHOWING THEIR RANGE AND VARIATIONS FROM RAILROAD SURVEY.

Month.	7 A. M.					2 P. M.					9 P. M.					Mean.				
	1st Year.	2d Year.	3d Year.	Mean.	Range.	1st Year.	2d Year.	3d Year.	Mean.	Range.	1st Year.	2d Year.	3d Year.	Mean.	Range.	1st Year.	2d Year.	3d Year.	Mean.	Range.
Oct.	—114.6	—108.1	— 67.5	— 96.8	47.1	+ 40.7	+ 90.5	+111.9	+ 81.0	71.2	— 96.1	— 84.0	— 23.8	— 68.0	72.3	— 55.3	— 33.7	+ 7.6	— 27.1	62.9
Nov.	—118.7	— 69.2	—101.1	— 96.3	49.5	+ 24.3	+ 62.9	+ 58.8	+ 48.7	38.6	— 93.1	— 40.0	— 68.2	— 67.1	53.1	— 63.1	— 14.8	— 36.5	— 38.1	48.3
Dec.	—136.1	— 46.6	— 95.9	— 92.9	89.5	— 6.0	+ 53.5	+ 18.6	+ 22.0	59.5	—101.1	— 21.7	— 71.5	— 64.8	79.4	— 80.6	— 5.1	— 50.5	— 45.4	75.5
Jan.	—106.3	— 81.6	— 58.9	— 82.3	47.4	+ 16.3	+ 31.0	+ 34.0	+ 27.1	17.7	— 77.9	— 52.1	— 34.2	— 54.7	43.7	— 55.9	— 34.0	— 20.1	— 36.7	35.8
Feb.	— 72.6	+ 2.6	— 6.8	— 25.6	75.2	+ 48.0	+ 51.1	+ 77.2	+ 58.8	29.2	— 51.6	+25.3	+ 2.8	— 7.8	76.9	— 25.7	+26.7	+23.5	+ 8.2	52.4
Mar.	— 48.9	— 31.1	— 58.0	— 46.0	26.9	+ 60.3	+ 54.7	+ 68.9	+ 61.3	14.2	— 46.5	— 4.6	— 34.3	— 28.5	41.9	— 11.9	+ 6.1	— 8.3	— 4.7	18.0
Apr.	— 7.7	— 22.2	— 31.8	— 20.6	24.1	+ 94.3	+ 63.8	+ 72.5	+ 76.9	30.5	— 56.7	— 16.5	— 18.2	— 30.5	40.2	+ 9.8	+ 8.0	+ 8.1	+ 8.6	1.8
May	+ 7.4	— 28.4	— 27.8	— 16.3	35.8	+100.3	+ 78.7	+134.8	+104.6	56.1	— 54.4	— 24.8	— 17.8	— 32.3	36.6	+18.3	+ 7.9	+29.6	+18.6	21.7
June	+ 14.0	— 11.9	— 27.5	— 8.5	41.5	+129.3	+119.2	+120.8	+123.1	10.1	— 34.4	— 25.2	— 7.3	— 22.3	27.1	+36.7	+27.7	+28.3	+30.9	9.0
July	— 26.6	— 22.2	— 16.3	— 21.7	10.3	+129.6	+113.4	+105.8	+116.3	23.8	— 37.4	— 22.5	— 4.8	— 21.6	32.6	+22.3	+23.4	+28.2	+24.6	5.9
Aug.	— 49.2	— 41.6	+ 25.2	— 21.9	74.4	+138.7	+139.0	+154.1	+143.9	15.4	— 63.7	— 45.9	+53.2	— 18.8	116.9	+ 8.4	+16.6	+77.7	+34.2	69.3
Sept.	— 59.2	— 51.2	— 55.2	— 55.2	8.0	+107.3	+115.4	+111.3	+111.3	8.1	— 78.0	— 33.4	— 55.7	— 55.7	44.6	— 8.9	+ 9.8	+ 0.5	+ 0.5	18.7
Mean	— 59.9	— 42.6	— 43.5	— 48.7	17.3	+ 73.6	+ 81.1	+ 89.1	+ 81.3	15.5	— 65.9	— 28.8	— 23.3	— 39.3	42.6	— 17.2	+ 3.2	+ 7.3	— 2.2	24.5

TABLES OF

XX.

APPROXIMATE ERROR OF BAROMETRIC MEASUREMENTS BETWEEN SACRAMENTO AND COLFAX.

By Railroad Survey, 2399 feet.

Hour.	Jan.	Feb.	Mar.	April.	May.	June.	July.	Aug.	Sept.	Oct.	Nov.	Dec.	Mean of Year.
7 A. M.	−32	−19	− 4	+17	+30	+27	+24	+ 7	−26	−43	−37	−35	− 8
2 P. M.	+27	+30	+56	+67	+77	+86	+85	+80	+58	+54	+38	+29	+57
9 P. M.	−19	− 7	− 4	+19	+13	+10	+ 3	−13	−29	−38	−31	−23	−10
Mean of Day.	− 8	0	+16	+33	+39	+40	+37	+24	0	− 9	−10	− 8	+13

XXI.

APPROXIMATE ERROR OF BAROMETRIC MEASUREMENTS BETWEEN SACRAMENTO AND SUMMIT.

By Railroad Survey, 6989 feet.

Hour.	Jan.	Feb.	Mar.	April.	May.	June.	July.	Aug.	Sept.	Oct.	Nov.	Dec.	Mean of Year.
7 A. M.	−165	−100	−76	− 26	− 28	− 36	− 70	− 90	−136	−200	−200	−190	−110
2 P. M.	− 10	+ 54	+78	+106	+130	+146	+132	+126	+104	+ 80	+ 40	− 12	+ 81
9 P. M.	−125	− 58	−52	− 32	− 42	− 70	− 82	− 90	−124	−162	−156	−142	− 94
Mean of Day.	−100	− 35	−17	+ 16	+ 20	+ 13	− 7	− 18	− 52	− 94	−105	−115	− 41

XXII.

APPROXIMATE ERROR OF BAROMETRIC MEASUREMENTS BETWEEN COLFAX AND SUMMIT.

By Railroad Survey, 4590 feet.

Hour.	Jan.	Feb.	Mar.	April.	May.	June.	July.	Aug.	Sept.	Oct.	Nov.	Dec.	Mean of Year.
7 A. M.	−84	−45	−40	−24	− 16	− 14	− 22	− 30	− 56	−98	−96	−93	−51
2 P. M.	+28	+54	+62	+75	+100	+124	+122	+120	+112	+84	+50	+24	+80
9 P. M.	−58	−32	−30	−26	− 24	− 20	− 22	− 30	− 56	−70	−68	−66	−42
Mean of Day.	−38	− 8	− 3	+ 8	+ 20	+ 30	+ 26	+ 12	0	−28	−38	−45	− 5

XXIII.

CORRECTIONS TO BE APPLIED FOR EACH THOUSAND FEET FROM SEA–LEVEL TO 2400 FEET.

Hour.	Jan.	Feb.	Mar.	April.	May.	June.	July.	Aug.	Sept.	Oct.	Nov.	Dec.	Mean of Year.
7 A.M.	+13.3	+ 7.9	+ 1.7	− 7.1	−12.5	−11.2	−10.0	− 2.9	+10.8	+17.9	+15.4	+14.6	+ 3.3
8 "	+ 8.2	+ 2.5	− 4.0	− 12.3	− 17.4	− 16.6	− 15.0	− 9.1	+ 3.1	+ 9.6	+ 11.6	+ 10.7	− 1.6
9 "	+ 2.8	− 3.4	− 9.7	− 16.7	− 21.5	− 21.5	− 19.7	− 14.4	− 3.6	+ 1.0	+ 6.9	+ 5.7	− 6.1
10 "	− 3.5	− 7.0	− 14.2	− 20.5	− 25.0	− 25.7	− 23.7	− 19.0	− 9.5	− 6.4	+ 0.5	− 0.4	− 10.4
11 "	− 6.8	− 9.6	− 17.5	− 23.4	− 27.8	− 29.0	− 27.4	− 23.0	− 15.0	− 12.0	− 6.4	− 5.0	− 14.5
12 M.	− 9.2	− 11.0	− 20.0	− 25.6	− 29.6	− 31.8	− 30.4	− 26.5	− 19.6	− 17.0	− 12.3	− 8.5	− 18.6
1 P.M.	− 10.5	− 12.0	− 21.9	− 27.2	− 31.0	− 34.0	− 33.3	− 30.2	− 22.7	− 21.0	− 15.3	− 11.0	− 21.7
2 "	− 11.2	−12.5	−23.3	−27.9	−32.1	−35.8	−35.4	−33.3	−24.2	−22.5	−15.8	−12.1	−23.7
3 "	− 10.0	− 12.0	− 21.4	− 27.9	− 32.0	− 36.5	− 36.0	− 34.1	− 23.2	− 20.7	− 15.0	− 10.5	− 21.0
4 "	− 7.8	− 9.6	− 17.9	− 24.8	− 30.4	− 36.0	− 33.9	− 32.2	− 19.7	− 16.0	− 11.2	− 7.8	− 16.9
5 "	− 4.0	− 6.6	− 12.5	− 20.4	− 27.1	− 31.1	− 29.4	− 26.3	− 15.0	− 8.7	− 4.8	− 4.0	− 11.9
6 "	0	− 2.8	− 6.0	− 16.0	− 21.5	− 23.3	− 20.4	− 16.2	− 6.0	0	+ 3.5	+ 0.7	− 6.4
7 "	+ 2.1	+ 1.0	− 2.2	− 12.5	− 14.4	− 13.0	− 11.0	− 4.3	+ 4.5	+ 7.8	+ 8.9	+ 6.3	− 1.6
8 "	+ 5.2	+ 2.8	+ 0.4	− 9.3	− 8.0	− 6.4	− 5.0	+ 3.3	+ 9.5	+ 12.6	+ 11.5	+ 8.2	+ 2.0
9 "	+ 7.9	+ 2.9	+ 1.7	− 7.9	− 5.4	− 4.2	− 1.2	+ 5.4	+ 12.1	+ 15.8	+ 12.9	+ 9.6	+ 4.1
Mean of Day.	+ 3.3	0	− 6.6	− 13.7	− 16.2	− 16.7	− 15.4	− 10.0	0	+ 3.7	+ 4.2	+ 3.3	− 5.4

XXIV.

CORRECTIONS TO BE APPLIED FOR EACH THOUSAND FEET FROM SEA–LEVEL TO 7000 FEET.

Hour.	Jan.	Feb.	Mar.	April.	May.	June.	July.	Aug.	Sept.	Oct.	Nov.	Dec.	Mean of Year.
7 A.M.	+23.6	+14.3	+10.9	+ 3.7	+ 4.0	+ 5.1	+10.0	+12.9	+19.4	+28.6	+28.6	+ 27.1	+15.7
8 "	+ 21.9	+ 12.4	+ 8.7	+ 1.0	+ 1.5	+ 1.4	+ 6.6	+ 8.7	+ 16.2	+ 24.8	+ 26.4	+ 25.4	+ 13.3
9 "	+ 19.2	+ 9.6	+ 5.5	− 1.8	− 1.8	− 2.7	+ 2.3	+ 4.4	+ 11.1	+ 19.6	+ 22.1	+ 22.5	+ 9.4
10 "	+ 16.0	+ 6.6	+ 2.6	− 4.6	− 5.0	− 6.8	− 2.4	− 0.4	+ 4.8	+ 12.8	+ 16.9	+ 19.0	+ 5.3
11 "	+ 11.2	+ 2.6	− 1.0	− 7.5	− 8.7	− 10.7	− 7.3	− 5.5	− 1.5	+ 5.8	+ 9.0	+ 13.8	0
12 M.	+ 6.6	− 1.6	− 4.7	− 10.8	− 13.3	− 15.5	− 12.9	− 11.3	− 8.0	− 1.0	+ 1.9	+ 8.0	− 5.0
1 P.M.	+ 3.3	− 6.0	− 9.0	− 14.0	− 17.0	− 19.0	− 17.0	− 16.0	− 12.7	− 6.8	− 2.8	+ 4.0	− 9.0
2 "	+ 1.4	− 7.7	−11.3	−15.1	−18.6	−20.9	−18.9	−18.0	−14.9	−11.4	− 5.7	+ 1.7	−11.6
3 "	+ 3.2	− 6.3	− 9.5	− 13.0	− 18.2	− 21.6	− 19.1	− 18.4	− 15.2	− 9.2	− 2.8	+ 3.8	− 9.8
4 "	+ 7.3	− 3.4	− 6.7	− 9.6	− 14.3	− 20.0	− 16.2	− 15.0	− 11.1	− 5.4	+ 1.8	+ 8.6	− 5.7
5 "	+ 11.1	+ 0.2	− 3.1	− 5.8	− 8.8	− 15.4	− 10.7	− 9.1	− 4.0	+ 0.4	+ 7.0	+ 12.6	− 0.4
6 "	+ 14.4	+ 3.0	+ 0.4	− 2.2	− 3.4	− 9.7	− 4.5	− 2.5	+ 5.0	+ 8.3	+ 12.2	+ 15.5	+ 5.1
7 "	+ 16.3	+ 5.4	+ 3.5	+ 0.8	+ 1.2	− 2.0	+ 1.8	+ 4.0	+ 12.5	+ 16.5	+ 17.5	+ 18.0	+ 9.1
8 "	+ 17.2	+ 7.3	+ 6.0	+ 3.5	+ 4.6	+ 5.3	+ 8.0	+ 9.6	+ 16.5	+ 21.6	+ 21.3	+ 19.5	+ 12.2
9 "	+ 17.9	+ 8.3	+ 7.4	+ 4.6	+ 6.0	+10.0	+ 11.7	+12.9	+17.7	+23.1	+22.3	+20.3	+13.4
Mean of Day	+ 14.3	+ 5.0	+ 2.4	− 2.3	− 2.9	− 1.9	+ 1.0	+ 2.6	+ 7.4	+13.4	+15.0	+16.4	+ 5.9

XXV.

CORRECTIONS TO BE APPLIED FOR EACH THOUSAND FEET OF DIFFERENCE OF LEVEL BETWEEN THE ALTITUDES OF 2400 AND 7000 FEET.

Hour.	Jan.	Feb.	Mar.	April.	May.	June.	July.	Aug.	Sept.	Oct.	Nov.	Dec.	Mean of Year.
7 A.M.	+18.3	+ 9.8	+ 8.7	+ 5.2	+ 3.5	+ 3.0	+ 4.8	+ 6.5	+12.2	+21.3	+20.9	+20.2	+ 11.1
8 "	+ 16.4	+ 7.6	+ 5.5	+ 2.5	+ 0.7	− 1.0	+ 1.0	+ 3.0	+ 8.7	+ 17.0	+ 17.8	+ 18.0	+ 8.0
9 "	+ 13.7	+ 4.9	+ 2.3	− 0.6	− 3.0	− 5.0	− 2.8	− 1.0	+ 4.4	+ 11.0	+ 14.6	+ 15.5	+ 3.8
10 "	+ 10.3	+ 1.7	− 1.2	− 3.9	− 7.0	− 9.6	− 7.3	− 5.5	− 0.3	+ 3.6	+ 9.8	+ 12.1	− 0.5
11 "	+ 6.2	− 2.3	− 5.3	− 7.6	− 11.0	− 14.5	− 12.6	− 10.3	− 6.1	− 4.0	+ 4.0	+ 7.8	− 5.4
12 M.	+ 0.4	− 7.3	− 10.0	− 11.5	− 15.7	− 20.7	− 19.4	− 17.0	− 14.5	− 11.0	− 3.5	+ 1.5	− 11.6
1 P.M.	− 4.7	− 10.9	− 12.1	− 15.1	− 20.4	− 25.5	− 24.7	− 24.0	− 22.2	− 16.7	− 10.2	− 3.9	− 16.1
2 "	− 6.1	− 11.7	−13.5	−16.3	−21.7	−27.0	−26.5	−26.1	−24.3	−18.3	−10.9	− 5.2	−17.4
3 "	− 3.5	− 9.3	− 11.4	− 14.0	− 21.0	− 27.4	− 26.3	− 25.0	− 22.1	− 15.0	− 7.0	− 2.0	− 15.0
4 "	+ 0.6	− 5.4	− 7.8	− 10.7	− 17.3	− 23.5	− 22.0	− 19.4	− 16.3	− 9.4	− 1.7	+ 2.0	− 10.7
5 "	+ 5.2	− 1.0	− 3.7	− 7.0	− 12.4	− 16.8	− 15.0	− 13.3	− 9.6	− 2.5	+ 4.0	+ 6.4	− 6.0
6 "	+ 9.4	+ 2.8	− 0.7	− 3.4	− 7.0	− 10.4	− 8.5	− 7.1	− 2.0	+ 4.5	+ 8.0	+ 10.3	− 0.9
7 "	+ 11.7	+ 5.7	+ 2.4	0	− 2.0	− 4.3	− 3.0	− 2.0	+ 5.0	+ 10.2	+ 11.6	+ 12.5	+ 3.7
8 "	+ 12.5	+ 6.8	+ 5.0	+ 3.3	+ 2.6	+ 0.8	+ 1.8	+ 3.4	+ 10.2	+ 14.5	+ 13.4	+ 13.8	+ 7.3
9 "	+12.6	+ 7.0	+ 6.5	+ 5.7	+ 5.2	+ 4.3	+ 4.8	+ 6.5	+12.2	+15.2	+14.8	+14.3	+ 9.1
Mean of Day.	+ 8.3	+ 1.7	+ 0.7	− 1.7	− 4.3	− 6.5	− 5.7	− 4.3	0	+ 6.1	+ 8.3	+ 9.8	+ 1.1

(UNIFORM WITH THE PUBLICATIONS OF THE)

GEOLOGICAL SURVEY OF CALIFORNIA.

J. D. WHITNEY, STATE GEOLOGIST.

CONTRIBUTIONS

TO

BAROMETRIC HYPSOMETRY:

WITH TABLES FOR USE
IN CALIFORNIA.

SUPPLEMENTARY CHAPTER:

A PRACTICAL APPLICATION OF THE TABLES TO THE OBSERVATIONS
OF THE YEARS 1870–71, AND A DISCUSSION OF
THE RESULTS OBTAINED.

CAMBRIDGE, MASS. :
PRINTED AT THE UNIVERSITY PRESS.
1878.

ERRATUM.

Page 80, Table XI., 4th line, last column, under "Mean," for —108.8, read —98.8.

SUPPLEMENTARY CHAPTER.

(October, 1878.)

SINCE the publication of the three preceding chapters, with the accompanying tables, the task of computing the altitudes of several hundred points, at which barometric observations were taken by the different field parties of the California survey during the seasons of 1870 and 1871, has been completed. The work has been pushed to a conclusion as rapidly as circumstances would allow, but progress has been of necessity slow, for a great part of the labor has had to be performed at such times only as could be spared from regular college duties.

The present chapter is intended to illustrate more fully than has heretofore been possible the practical value of the special tables of corrections prepared for use in California, and to show to what extent their use will be of advantage in securing a closer approximation to the truth than can be hoped for without them; especially in cases where only single observations or, at best, short series of observations are available. The examples chosen for purposes of illustration have all been taken from the work of the years 1870 and 1871, for the reason that during those years barometric observations were taken more systematically and thoroughly than they have been either before or since in the history of the survey, and the observations have been reduced with particular reference to the problem at present under discussion.

There were three active field parties engaged on the work of the survey in 1870 : one was in the field from the first of May to the first of August, occupied for the most part in Owen's Valley, and the mountainous region of Inyo and Mono counties; a second spent the months of September, October, and November in the neighborhood of Clear Lake, in the Coast Ranges, north of the Bay of San Francisco; and a third was employed from early in the season until the month of December in the auriferous gravel districts of Yuba, Nevada, and Placer counties. The organization of the first two parties was essentially the same, Messrs. Hoffmann and Craven being in charge of the topographical part of the work, and Mr. Goodyear of the geological; Mr. Rabe was an efficient aid in the barometric work. The field-work in the gravel district was begun in May by Mr. Bowman, who was joined early in July by Mr. Pettee. Several other persons, not otherwise connected with the survey, gave valuable assistance in the barometric work from time to time at places where it was found convenient to establish stations of reference as the work progressed. The field-work of 1871 was confined almost exclusively to Mr. Goodyear's examination of the gravel districts of Placer, El Dorado, and Amador counties. The barometers in use were all mercurial cistern barometers, made by James Green of New York.

The number of different points at which observations for the determination of altitude were taken was a little more than seven hundred, but the total number of separate computations, which have been made in the course of the work, amounts to over two thousand. Each computation has been made by itself without regard to others, for the sake of bringing into prominence, as far as possible, the effects of times and seasons upon the final results. The method employed was as follows. The barometric data for each computation were first freed from instrumental errors and reduced to a common standard. Then followed the computation according to Williamson's tables, no account being taken of the moisture in the atmosphere. The corrections for temperature, for latitude, and for the decrease of gravity were all made in the usual order. This led to what has been regarded heretofore as the final and best result obtainable from the data employed. In what follows in this chapter this result will be called the *uncorrected result,* or the *uncorrected difference of altitude.* The next step was to apply an additional correction derived from the new tables. In deciding upon the proper value to be assigned to this correction in particular cases there was occasionally some ground for doubt and a difference of opinion, the tables not being sufficiently extensive to meet all requirements. Having been prepared from observations taken at only three stations, Sacramento, Colfax, and Summit, they cannot be expected to furnish precise corrections for other places. For instance, when one of the two stations involved in a computation was Sacramento, and the other was a point midway in altitude between Colfax and

Summit, the question would arise whether the Sacramento-Colfax (XXIII.), or the Sacramento-Summit (XXIV.) table was to be preferred. In other cases doubts would arise from the fact that both the field station, and the corresponding station which was in all other respects the best for reference, were considerably different in altitude from either Sacramento, Colfax, or Summit. Furthermore, the tables, being based upon monthly averages, must be looked upon as strictly applicable to the middle portions of each month only. These difficulties were overcome, sometimes in one way and sometimes in another, but always with a view of getting that value for the correction which was the most probable, after taking into account all the circumstances and conditions which could affect it. Fortunately, the amount of error in the final results, dependent upon any uncertainty which might attach to the determination of the value of this correction, is in no case of material importance. The quantities involved are neither absolutely nor relatively large. In all the numerical work every precaution was taken to secure accuracy, and it is hoped that no important error has escaped correction.

For each one of about four hundred points, out of the seven hundred visited, only a single computation for altitude has been made, either for the reason that only one observation was taken at the field station, or because the several observations taken were so related to each other, and to the records at the corresponding stations, that only one really independent computation was practicable. The cases of this class are, of course, of no value in illustrating the use of the new tables.

In one hundred and forty-six cases computations have been made to show the differences of altitude between the field station and *two or more corresponding stations*, the altitudes of which have been determined by accurate spirit-level surveys, or from barometric observations extending, with a few exceptions, over considerable intervals of time. If the tables in ordinary use gave accurate results, it is evident that the calculated altitudes above the level of the sea of any one of these one hundred and forty-six stations ought to be the same, whatever point might be chosen as corresponding station or station of reference. For example, the calculated altitude of Lowell Hill ought to be the same, whether the corresponding station barometer was observed at Colfax or at Summit. As a matter of fact, in this particular example the uncorrected results, obtained in the usual way, differed from each other by 118.6 feet.   The corrected results differed by only 29.2 feet.   This comparatively close agreement of the results obtained by the use of the new tables is, as far as it goes, a good piece of evidence in their favor, and shows that either one of the corrected results, taken by itself, is probably considerably nearer the truth than either of the uncorrected ones.   It would extend this chapter to an unreasonable length to give the details of all the cases which bear upon this phase of the subject.   For the purposes of illustration the cases cited in the following table have been chosen.   The column in the table headed " Uncorrected Results " contains the computed altitudes of the field stations above the sea, determined independently of each other, and without the use of the new tables.   The column of " Corrected Results " gives the final determinations of altitude after the application of the corrections. The columns of " Differences " show, at a glance, how great the disagreement is in each case.

ALTITUDES COMPUTED WITH REFERENCE TO DIFFERENT CORRESPONDING STATIONS.

	Field Station.	Corresponding Stations.	Uncorrected Results.	Difference.	Corrected Results.	Difference.
1	McKune's.	Smartsville ...	3006.0	75.7	2941.0	10.7
		Nevada City..	2930.3		2930.3	
2	Summit of road on Pet Hill.	Smartsville ...	1641.6	20.4	1624.4	13.5
		Nevada City..	1621.2		1637.9	
3	" Lava Castle."	Colfax	6621.0	135.8	6530.6	13.7
		Summit	6485.2		6516.9	
4	Lava Summit near Liberty Hill.	Colfax	4472.7	25.4	4463.9	5.4
		Summit	4447.3		4458.4	
5	Reed's.	Colfax	393.6	60.2	418.0	30.7
		Sacramento...	453.8		448.7	
6	Camp 60 (Inyo trip).	Dutch Flat ...	5151.4	36.1	5164.4	19.5
		Summit	5187.5		5183.9	
7	Camp 11 (Kelsey Creek).	Colfax	1398.2	26.9	1392.7	17.5
		Sacramento...	1371.3		1375.2	

	Field Station.	Corresponding Stations.	Uncorrected Results.	Difference.	Corrected Results.	Difference.
8	Camp 20 (Bear Valley).	Colfax	1402.1	68.5	1388.9	38.5
		Sacramento ...	1333.6		1350.4	
9	Secret House.	Colfax	5503.6	132.5	5440.0	34.7
		Summit........	5371.1		5405.3	
10	Crest of ridge back of Startown.	Colfax	4908.4	94.4	4868.0	5.8
		Summit	4814.0		4873.8	
11	Ford's Bar.	Colfax	796.8	115.7	845.0	41.4
		Sacramento...	912.5		886.4	
12	Big Trees, above Last Chance.	Colfax	5287.8	136.5	5215.7	17.4
		Summit........	5151.3		5198.3	
13	Wilcox's Meadows.	Georgetown...	5398.7	84.8	5332.1	23.1
		Summit........	5313.9		5355.2	
14	Marble Valley.	Colfax	889.2	63.3	911.7	27.3
		Sacramento ...	952.5		939.0	
15	Mule Cañon.	Colfax	2832.2	16.8	2833.0	29.0
		Morison's.....	2815.4		2804.0	
16	Klipstein's.	Colfax	4138.9	19.1	4173.8	113.2
		Summit	4119.8		4060.6	
17	Bridge near Leavitt's.	Nevada City..	5717.0	3.7	5632.5	21.9
		Dutch Flat ...	5720.7		5654.4	
18	Point on Cosumnes River.	Colfax	1685.0	9.7	1699.1	55.3
		Sacramento ...	1675.3		1643.8	

With one exception the results given in this table are based upon one or at most two observations only. The exception is No. 7, that of Camp 11 on Kelsey Creek, for which point the altitudes given are the means derived from forty independent computations for both Sacramento and Colfax. The observations used in the computations were those taken at 9 P. M., October 1st, and at 7 A. M., 2 P. M., and 9 P. M. from the 2d to the 12th inclusive, and on the 16th and 17th. That is to say, they represent very nearly the daily means for the first half of the month of October. With a series of observations so extensive as this, it would seem as if a still closer accordance might be expected, but there were among the eighty results a few of an abnormal character for which no explanation can be given. They may have been due to a lack of care on the part of the observers, but they are not so obviously erroneous as to justify their rejection.

An inspection of the columns of differences shows very plainly that, in the first fourteen cases cited, the use of the new tables has brought widely discordant results into a considerably closer agreement. Absolute identity in computations of this kind will not be looked for by any one familiar with the subject. Even under the most favorable circumstances there are liable to be local peculiarities, at one or at both of the stations, which will have an influence upon the barometer or thermometer, for which no allowance can be made; or small undetected errors in the reading of the scales on the instruments will be magnified in the numerical work which follows; and unless a record is kept of all the more important meteorological phenomena, especially of the direction and force of the wind, and of the presence or absence of clouds, in connection with the ordinary observations for barometric pressure and for temperature, the computer will be in no position to judge whether the corrections, particularly that for temperature, which is almost always much the largest of them all, are overestimated or underestimated.

Not unfrequently, indeed, the atmospheric or local conditions are decidedly unfavorable for the accurate determination of altitudes with the barometer. If the day is warm, and the sky is bright and clear at one station, while at the other a gathering thunder-storm causes a rapid cooling of the atmosphere, it is evident that the readings of the thermometers at the two stations do not furnish sufficient data to enable one to form any just estimate of the mean temperature of the intervening air column. It will not be a matter of surprise, therefore, that the uncorrected results sometimes agree with each other even more closely than the corrected ones do. The cases numbered from 15 to 18 in the table are of this character. Of course no provision can be made in tables of corrections for such emergencies, and if it had been found, as the result of the examination of a large number of cases, that the use of such tables led as often or to as great an extent to the increase of discrepancies as it did to their removal, there would certainly be little to hope for in carrying the investigation further in this direction. In thirty-six of the one hundred and forty-six cases now under consideration, or nearly twenty-five per cent, the use of the new tables of corrections increases to a greater or less extent (in one or two instances quite largely) the discrepancies in the computed results. This number is so large that it would afford a reasonable basis for doubt as to the general trustworthiness of the tables, unless it could be shown that there was something abnormal or out of the usual course in the original observations or in the accompanying circumstances.

In five of these thirty-six unfavorable cases the field stations were in Mono County, while the corresponding stations were at Nevada City and Dutch Flat, — points hardly twelve miles apart, but about a hundred miles distant from the field stations, and on the opposite slope of the Sierra Nevada Mountains. (See No. 17 in the table.) The tables of corrections are surely not chargeable with failure under conditions so radically different from those for which they were calculated. In five other cases, one of which is No. 16 in the table, the field observations were taken on the 25th and 26th of November, just at the beginning of what proved to be a long and severe snow-storm. Probably the atmospheric disturbance was already so far advanced as to affect materially any computations based upon a formula which presupposes a condition of atmospheric equilibrium. In four cases, one of which is No. 15 in the table, either the field station or one of the corresponding stations was near the border of Clear Lake, a sheet of water having an area, approximately, of a hundred square miles. It is not unreasonable to suppose that this large body of water, nearly surrounded by mountains, some of which rise to a height of from two to three thousand feet above the level of the lake, will have such an influence upon the atmosphere as to vitiate to some extent the accuracy of barometric calculations. No numerical value can be assigned to this disturbing factor. In some of the remaining cases there were special peculiarities, which possibly had some influence upon the computed results, and there are only six or eight cases left which baffle all attempts at explanation.

Taking the one hundred and ten favorable cases by themselves, the average difference of the uncorrected results is 55.0 feet, and that of the corrected results is 19.1 feet, a reduction of about sixty-five per cent. The average difference of the uncorrected results in the thirty-six unfavorable cases is

17.2 feet, while that of the corrected results is 36.6 feet, the difference being a little more than doubled. Combining the favorable and the unfavorable cases, these numbers become, respectively, 45.7 and 23.5, showing that on the average *the new tables, when applied to observations taken in Central California, may be expected to reduce such discrepancies by about one half.*

There now remains one more important group of computations to be examined. At a great many points visited by the different parties in the field, a series of barometric observations was taken. In some instances the series embraced hourly observations for several days in succession, and in others observations were taken at less frequent intervals, though extending over several days. In the majority of cases the series was short, comprising only two or three observations taken at different hours of the same day, or on different days. The larger part of these observations could not be made directly useful in the subsequent computations, for the reason that there were no synchronous, or nearly synchronous observations to compare with at any convenient corresponding station; but in all cases where two or more observations were taken at any field station, far enough apart in time to be regarded as independent of each other, for which suitable corresponding observations could be found, as many independent computations as possible were made to determine the difference of altitude between the field station and the corresponding station selected for reference. There were in all one hundred and seventy-one such cases. In one case as many as forty-five independent computations were made; in seventeen cases the number of computations was twenty or more; and there were fifty-seven cases for which there were at least five such computations. If the tables in ordinary use always gave accurate results, the several calculated differences of altitude for any given pair of stations ought to be equal to each other. If they are not equal, there is a source of error somewhere, which requires additional correction.

That there is a real advantage to be gained from the use of the new tables in these cases may be made to appear in two ways. The application of the corrections ought to diminish all such uncorrected differences of altitude as are already too high, and to increase such as are too low, provided there is nothing abnormal in any of the observations which form the basis of the computation. The *range* of the corrected differences of the altitude, or the absolute difference between the highest and the lowest of the several determinations, therefore, ought to be less than that of the uncorrected differences. When the test is applied in this form to the one hundred and seventy-one cases now under consideration, it is found that the result is favorable in two thirds of the instances, and unfavorable in the remaining one third. But this method of testing the value of the tables is imperfect. It not unfrequently happens that just those values of the uncorrected differences of altitude which are farthest from the mean or true value are those which are abnormal in character; and hence the application of the corrections, although it may bring the most of the results into closer harmony, will at the same time cause an increase in the range, or extreme variation from the mean value.

The other method of estimating the worth of the new tables is more satisfactory. An examination is made of all the separate results in detail, for the purpose of ascertaining in how many instances the application of the corrections has caused the uncorrected difference of altitude to approach the true value when known, or the mean of all the corrected determinations (which, in the absence of anything more definite, will have to be accepted as the best approximation to the truth), and in how many cases the reverse holds true.

The table on the following pages gives the details of a number of cases selected to illustrate these two methods. The columns headed I. and II. contain respectively the several computed differences of altitude (with their range) between the field stations and the corresponding stations before and after the application of the corrections from the new tables. Column III. contains the variations of the uncorrected results from the known difference of altitude between the stations, as in No. 3 (Blue Cañon and Summit) and in No. 7 (Gold Run and Colfax), or from the mean of the corrected results, which is assumed to be a close approximation to the truth, when the true difference is not known from other sources. Column IV. contains similarly the variations of the corrected results. The numbers in column IV. will be smaller than the corresponding numbers in column III., whenever the application of the correction has diminished the error of the uncorrected result, and larger, whenever the error has been increased.

TABLE SHOWING THE RANGE AND THE ERRORS OF THE UNCORRECTED AND THE CORRECTED DIFFERENCES OF ALTITUDE BETWEEN TWO STATIONS.

	Field Station.	Corresponding Station.	Date.			I. Uncorrected.	Range.	II. Corrected.	Range.	III. Uncorrected.	IV. Corrected.
1	Riley Lane's.	Smartsville	May 25	9 P.M.		628.0	5.0	624.7	0.5	3.0	0.3
			" 26	7 A.M.		633.0		625.2		8.0	0.2
				Mean		630.5		625.0		5.5	0.3
2	Tompkins's.	Smartsville	June 20	9^{10} P.M.		3806.4	41.0	3817.4	18.0	20.0	9.0
			" 21	7 A.M.		3847.4		3835.4		21.0	9.0
				Mean		3826.9		3826.4		20.5	9.0
3	Blue Cañon.	Summit.	Aug. 13	2^{25} P.M.		2371.0		2310.0		34.9	26.1
			Sept. 12	7^{30} A.M.		2296.0	93.2	2319.0	35.2	40.1	17.1
			" 12	12^{30} P.M.		2389.2		2345.2		53.1	9.1
			" 12	6^{15} P.M.		2312.0		2312.0		24.1	24.1
				Mean		2342.0		2321.5		38.0	19.1
4	Murphy's.	Summit.	Aug. 27	7^{30} A.M.		4805.5		4841.5		17.1	18.9
			" 27	2 P.M.		4952.5	212.3	4827.3	57.2	129.9	4.7
			" 27	9 P.M.		4740.2		4784.3		82.4	38.3
			" 29	7 A.M.		4792.6		4837.2		30.0	14.6
				Mean		4822.7		4822.6		64.8	19.1
5	Columbia.	Summit.	Aug. 30	7 A.M.		4833.9		4878.8		26.0	18.9
			" 30	2 P.M.		5001.9	216.3	4875.9	48.7	142.0	16.0
			" 30	9 P.M.		4785.6		4830.1		74.3	29.8
			" 31	7 A.M.		4810.0		4854.8		49.9	5.1
				Mean		4857.8		4859.9		73.0	17.4
6	Dutch Flat Hotel.	Colfax.	Oct. 27	2 P.M.		757.3		746.3		12.3	1.3
			" 27	9 P.M.		734.8	29.8	745.9	3.5	10.2	0.9
			" 28	7 A.M.		727.5		742.8		17.5	2.2
				Mean		739.9		745.0		13.3	1.5

Field Station.	Corresponding Station.	Date.			I. Uncorrected	Range.	II. Corrected.	Range.	III. Uncorrected.	IV. Corrected.
7 Gold Run.	Colfax.	Oct.	7	7 A.M.	787.5		804.2		22.0	5.3
		"	7	2 P.M.	829.5		814.3		20.0	4.8
		"	7	9 P.M.	790.5		802.5		19.0	7.0
		"	8	7 A.M.	795.6		812.6		13.9	3.1
		"	9	2 P.M.	835.7		820.5		26.2	11.0
		"	9	9 P.M.	792.1		804.3		17.4	5.2
		"	10	7 A.M.	790.9		807.9		18.6	1.6
		"	10	2 P.M.	829.1		813.9		19.6	4.4
		"	11	7 A.M.	795.3	56.6	812.3	29.8	14.2	2.8
		"	11	3^{30} P.M.	829.7		819.7		20.2	10.2
		"	11	9 P.M.	780.9		792.7		28.6	16.8
		"	12	7 A.M.	799.1		816.1		10.4	6.6
		"	12	2 P.M.	827.9		812.7		18.4	3.2
		"	12	9 P.M.	789.4		801.4		20.1	8.1
		"	13	7 A.M.	779.1		796.7		30.4	12.8
		"	13	2 P.M.	824.7		809.6		15.2	0.1
		"	13	9 P.M.	791.9		803.9		17.6	5.6
				Mean	804.1		808.5		19.5	6.4
8 Nevada City.	Smartsville	July	14	10^{25} A.M.	1740.6		1696.0		22.2	22.4
		"	14	2 P.M.	1780.9		1717.9		62.5	0.5
		"	14	7 P.M.	1719.6		1700.7		1.2	17.7
		"	15	7 A.M.	1786.2		1768.3		67.8	49.9
		"	15	2 P.M.	1790.5		1727.5		72.1	9.1
		"	15	7 P.M.	1766.2		1746.8		47.8	28.4
		"	16	2 P.M.	1784.5		1721.5		66.1	3.1
		"	16	7 P.M.	1703.5	99.1	1684.8	94.2	14.9	33.6
		"	17	7 A.M.	1730.1		1712.8		11.7	5.6
		"	18	2 P.M.	1802.6		1738.9		84.2	20.5
		"	18	7 P.M.	1734.1		1715.0		15.7	3.4
		"	19	7 A.M.	1716.6		1699.4		1.8	19.0
		"	19	2 P.M.	1735.4		1674.1		17.0	44.3
		"	19	7 P.M.	1765.8		1746.4		47.4	28.0
		"	20	7 A.M.	1742.7		1725.3		24.3	6.9
				Mean	1753.3		1718.4		37.1	19.5
9 Nevada City.	Dutch Flat	July	27	7 A.M.	690.8		694.7		16.1	20.0
		"	28	2 P.M.	682.7		664.7		8.0	10.0

Field Station.	Corresponding Station.	Date.			I. Uncorrected.	Range.	II. Corrected.	Range.	III. Uncorrected.	IV. Corrected.
9 Nevada City (Continued).	Dutch Flat	July	29	7 A.M.	700.7		704.6		26.0	29.9
		"	29	2 P.M.	685.9		667.9		11.2	6.8
		"	29	7 P.M.	676.9		675.2		2.2	0.5
		"	30	7 A.M.	669.0		672.7		5.7	2.0
		"	30	2 P.M.	682.1		664.1		7.4	10.6
		"	30	7 P.M.	665.7		667.4		9.0	7.3
		"	31	7 A.M.	667.0		670.7		7.7	4.0
		"	31	2 P.M.	671.3		653.7		3.4	21.0
		Aug.	1	7 A.M.	664.3		668.0		10.4	6.7
		"	1	2 P.M.	690.4		672.3		15.7	2.4
		"	1	7 P.M.	680.1		681.8		5.4	7.1
		"	2	7 A.M.	678.0	49.3	681.7	58.2	3.3	7.0
		"	2	2 P.M.	682.5		664.6		7.8	10.1
		"	2	7 P.M.	667.9		666.2		6.8	8.5
		"	3	7^{30} A.M.	676.6		680.3		1.9	5.6
		"	3	2 P.M.	694.5		676.3		19.8	1.6
		"	3	7 P.M.	666.0		664.3		8.7	10.4
		"	4	7 A.M.	664.7		668.4		10.0	6.3
		"	4	2 P.M.	694.3		678.1		19.6	3.4
		"	4	7 P.M.	672.6		670.9		2.1	3.8
		"	5	7 A.M.	673.1		676.8		1.6	2.1
		"	5	2 P.M.	678.6		660.8		3.9	13.9
		"	5	7 P.M.	713.6		711.9		38.9	37.2
		"	6	8 A.M.	666.3		667.6		8.4	7.1
		"	6	2 P.M.	697.7		679.4		23.0	4.7
		"	6	7 P.M.	689.3		687.6		14.6	12.9
				Mean	680.1		674.7		10.7	9.4
10 You Bet.	Colfax.	Nov.	10	9 P.M.	576.4		585.3		19.0	27.9
		"	11	7 A.M.	552.7		564.5		4.7	7.1
		"	11	1^{45} P.M.	583.2		572.5		25.8	15.1
		"	11	7^{25} P.M.	561.1		568.3		3.7	10.9
		"	12	7 A.M.	585.4		597.9		28.0	40.5
		"	16	2 P.M.	568.5		562.2		11.1	4.8
		"	16	9 P.M.	532.5		540.6		24.9	16.8
		"	17	7 A.M.	539.5		551.0		17.9	6.4
		"	17	1 P.M.	558.7		552.8		1.3	4.6
		"	18	2 P.M.	557.1		550.8		0.3	6.6
		"	19	2 P.M.	565.7		559.4		7.3	2.0

Field Station.	Corresponding Station.	Date.			I. Uncorrected	Range.	II. Corrected.	Range.	III. Uncorrected.	IV. Corrected.
10 You Bet (Continued).	Colfax.	Nov.	20	7³⁰ A.M.	546.8	57.0	557.6	58.0	10.6	0.2
		"	20	2 P.M.	550.7		544.5		6.7	12.9
		"	20	9 P.M.	534.7		542.8		22.7	14.6
		"	21	7 A.M.	537.8		549.3		19.6	8.1
		"	21	2 P.M.	564.2		557.9		6.8	0.5
		"	21	9 P.M.	532.5		540.6		24.9	16.8
		"	22	7 A.M.	528.4		539.9		29.0	17.5
		"	23	7 A.M.	538.4		549.9		19.0	7.5
		Dec.	8	2 P.M.	566.3		563.2		8.9	5.8
		"	8	9 P.M.	556.8		564.0		0.8	6.6
		"	9	7 A.M.	541.6		553.1		15.8	4.3
		"	12	7 A.M.	546.4		557.9		11.0	0.5
		"	12	7 P.M.	544.8		551.7		12.6	5.7
				Mean	552.9		557.4		13.8	10.2
11 Lone Pine.	Smartsville	May	17	7 A.M.	3113.4		3125.9		68.7	56.2
		"	17	9³⁵ A.M.	3184.8		3174.0		2.7	8.1
		"	17	1 P.M.	3278.7		3223.0		96.6	40.9
		"	17	6⁴⁵ P.M.	3239.5		3239.5		57.4	57.4
		"	17	9 P.M.	3159.1		3178.1		23.0	4.0
		"	18	7 A.M.	3102.7		3115.2		79.4	66.9
		"	18	12³⁰ P.M.	3240.9		3191.6		58.8	9.5
		"	18	9 P.M.	3186.5		3205.6		4.4	23.5
		"	19	7 A.M.	3169.1		3181.7		13.0	0.4
		"	19	9 A.M.	3208.8		3203.0		26.7	20.9
		"	19	12 M.	3267.5		3224.2		85.4	42.1
		"	19	2³⁰ P.M.	3255.1		3195.3		73.0	13.2
		"	19	9 P.M.	3232.5		3251.9		50.4	69.8
		"	20	7³⁰ A.M.	3261.0		3270.1		78.9	88.0
		"	20	3³⁰ P.M.	3283.1		3229.7		101.0	47.6
		"	20	9 P.M.	3177.3		3196.4		4.8	14.3
		"	21	7 A.M.	3156.2		3143.5		25.9	38.6
		"	21	9 A.M.	3203.7		3197.9		21.6	15.8
		"	21	12 M.	3270.9	219.7	3227.6	194.4	88.8	45.5
		"	21	2 P.M.	3279.2		3218.3		97.1	36.2
		"	21	4 P.M.	3280.1		3233.3		98.0	51.2
		"	21	9 P.M.	3125.6		3144.3		56.5	37.8
		"	22	7 P.M.	3160.4		3164.2		21.7	17.9
		"	22	9 P.M.	3130.2		3148.9		51.9	33.2

Field Station.	Correspond-ing Station.	Date.			I.		II.		III.	IV.
					Uncor-rected.	Range.	Cor-rected.	Range.	Uncor-rected.	Cor-rected.
11 Lone Pine. (*Continued*).	Smartsville	May	23	7 A.M.	3074.2		3086.5		107.9	95.6
		"	23	9 P.M.	3135.4		3154.1		46.7	28.0
		"	24	7 A.M.	3063.4		3075.7		118.7	106.4
		"	24	12 M.	3225.2		3181.9		43.1	0.2
		"	24	2 P.M.	3233.1		3173.0		51.0	9.1
		"	24	4 P.M.	3232.9		3176.7		50.8	5.4
		"	24	9 P.M.	3141.4		3160.3		40.7	21.8
		"	25	7 A.M.	3103.4		3115.8		78.7	66.3
		"	25	9 A.M.	3160.6		3154.9		21.5	27.2
		"	25	12 M.	3245.3		3202.0		63.2	19.9
		"	25	2 P.M.	3232.6		3172.5		50.5	9.6
		"	25	9 P.M.	3135.6		3154.4		46.5	27.7
		"	26	7 A.M.	3175.1		3187.8		7.0	5.7
		"	26	9²⁰ A.M.	3251.7		3242.6		69.6	60.5
			Mean		3194.1		3182.1		54.8	34.8
12 Bend City.	Smartsville	May	28	7²⁵ A.M.	3088.2		3092.8		6.1	10.7
		"	28	9 A.M.	3184.8		3172.1		102.7	90.0
		"	28	2 P.M.	3307.7		3227.5		225.6	145.4
		"	28	4 P.M.	3324.3		3256.4		242.2	174.3
		"	28	9 P.M.	3200.6		3215.6		118.5	133.5
		"	29	7³⁰ A.M.	3296.4		3301.3		214.3	219.2
		"	30	12 M.	3178.5		3120.7		96.4	38.6
		"	30	2 P.M.	3162.0		3085.2		79.9	3.1
		"	30	4 P.M.	3191.3		3126.1		109.2	44.0
		"	30	9 P.M.	3121.3		3106.6		39.2	24.5
		"	31	7 A.M.	3051.9		3061.7		30.2	20.4
		"	31	8³⁰ A.M.	3097.6		3091.1		15.5	9.0
		"	31	2 P.M.	3216.5		3138.7		134.4	56.6
		"	31	7 P.M.	3043.7		3034.3		38.4	47.8
		June	1	7 A.M.	3032.9		3042.6		49.2	39.5
		"	1	8¹⁵ A.M.	3075.5		3069.0		6.6	13.1
		"	1	11 A.M.	3111.8		3072.0		29.7	10.1
		"	1	12 M.	3125.5		3068.6		43.4	13.5
		"	1	2 P.M.	3154.5	388.3	3077.9	355.9	72.4	4.2
		"	1	4 P.M.	3149.2		3084.9		67.1	2.8
		"	1	9 P.M.	3075.0		3089.4		7.1	7.3
		"	2	7 A.M.	3034.5		3044.2		47.6	37.9
		"	2	9 A.M.	3165.7		3153.0		83.6	70.9

Field Station.	Corresponding Station.	Date.			I. Uncorrected	Range.	II. Corrected.	Range.	III. Uncorrected.	IV. Corrected.
12 Bend City (*Continued*).	Smartsville	June	2	2 P.M.	3148.9		3072.3		66.8	9.8
		"	2	4 P.M.	3034.2		2972.4		47.9	109.7
		"	2	8 P.M.	2994.8		2999.9		97.3	82.2
		"	3	7 A.M.	2963.0		2972.5		119.1	109.6
		"	3	10⁵⁰ A.M.	3063.4		3025.2		18.7	56.9
		"	3	12³⁰ P.M.	3095.5		3031.7		13.4	50.4
		"	3	4³⁰ P.M.	3117.4		3063.0		35.3	19.1
		"	4	7¹⁰ A.M.	2979.0		2988.5		103.1	93.6
		"	4	7 P.M.	3128.0		3118.3		45.9	36.2
		"	5	7 A.M.	2936.0		2945.4		146.1	136.7
		"	5	3¹⁵ P.M.	3166.0		3089.4		83.9	7.3
		"	6	7 A.M.	2984.1		2993.7		98.0	88.4
		"	6	3³⁰ P.M.	3138.7		3069.7		56.6	12.4
		"	6	9 P.M.	3032.2		3046.5		49.9	35.6
		"	7	7 A.M.	2988.8		2998.4		93.3	83.7
				Mean	3109.5		3082.1		77.2	56.5
13 Camp 37.	Smartsville	June	27	4 P.M.	5148.7		5031.4		281.5	164.2
		"	27	9 P.M.	4929.1		4951.3		61.9	84.1
		"	28	7 A.M.	4981.3		5000.7		114.1	133.5
		"	28	9 A.M.	5103.0		5083.1		235.8	215.9
		"	28	12 M.	5211.3		5107.1		344.1	239.9
		"	28	2 P.M.	5230.4		5090.7		363.2	223.5
		"	28	9 P.M.	4943.6		4965.8		76.4	98.6
		"	29	7 A.M.	4884.7		4903.7		17.5	36.5
		"	29	9 A.M.	4954.1		4934.8		86.9	67.6
		"	29	12 M.	5055.9		4954.7		188.7	87.5
		"	29	2 P.M.	5084.6		4950.8		217.4	83.6
		"	29	9 P.M.	4899.6		4921.7		32.4	54.5
		"	30	7 A.M.	4805.5		4824.2		61.7	43.0
		"	30	9⁴⁰ A.M.	4912.6		4878.2		45.4	11.0
		"	30	12 M.	4957.2		4858.1		90.0	9.1
		"	30	2 P.M.	4999.9		4866.4		132.7	0.8
		"	30	4 P.M.	4998.4		4884.9		131.2	17.7
		"	30	9 P.M.	4832.3		4854.4		34.9	12.8
		July	1	7 A.M.	4724.6	527.0	4743.0	385.4	142.6	124.2
		"	1	9 A.M.	4780.5		4761.9		86.7	105.3
		"	1	12¹⁵ P.M.	4892.9		4782.1		25.7	85.1
		"	1	2 P.M.	4948.5		4816.3		81.3	50.9
		"	1	4 P.M.	4976.4		4862.9		109.2	4.3

Field Station.	Corresponding Station.	Date.			I. Uncorrected	Range.	II. Corrected.	Range.	III. Uncorrected.	IV. Corrected.
13 Camp 37 (*Continued*).	Smartsville	July	1	9 P.M.	4836.4		4858.5		30.8	8.7
		"	2	7 A.M.	4716.4		4734.8		150.8	132.4
		"	2	9 A.M.	4804.7		4786.0		62.5	81.2
		"	2	12 M.	4874.0		4776.5		6.8	90.7
		"	2	2 P.M.	4902.2		4771.4		35.0	95.8
		"	2	4 P.M.	4910.3		4799.1		43.1	68.1
		"	2	9 P.M.	4751.6		4772.9		115.6	94.3
		"	3	7 A.M.	4703.4		4721.7		163.8	145.5
		"	3	9^{30} A.M.	4836.1		4806.1		31.1	61.1
		"	3	2^{35} P.M.	4925.6		4793.6		58.4	73.6
		"	3	9 P.M.	4802.8		4824.8		64.4	42.4
		"	4	7 A.M.	4722.3		4740.7		144.9	126.5
		"	4	1^{25} P.M.	4963.6		4834.9		96.4	32.3
		"	5	8 A.M.	4870.4		4870.4		3.2	3.2
		"	5	1^{30} P.M.	5005.4		4875.4		138.2	8.2
		"	5	9 P.M.	4804.0		4826.0		63.2	41.2
				Mean	4915.0		4867.2		106.9	78.4
14 Gregory Flat.	Smartsville	July	14	2 P.M.	6728.6		6550.4		200.1	21.9
		"	15	7 A.M.	6445.9		6476.9		82.6	51.6
		"	15	2^{30} P.M.	6764.7		6586.1		236.2	57.6
		"	15	9 P.M.	6465.7		6496.8		62.8	31.7
		"	16	7 A.M.	6491.0		6522.2		37.5	6.3
		"	16	2 P.M.	6751.6		6572.7		223.1	48.2
		"	16	9 P.M.	6456.3		6487.4		72.2	41.1
		"	17	7 A.M.	6465.5		6496.6		63.0	31.9
		"	18	7^{15} A.M.	6487.0		6511.6		41.5	16.9
		"	18	9^{30} A.M.	6585.4		6552.5		56.9	24.0
		"	18	2 P.M.	6785.0	372.6	6605.5	172.8	256.5	77.0
		"	18	4^{25} P.M.	6740.9		6616.0		212.4	87.5
		"	18	9 P.M.	6412.4		6443.2		116.1	85.3
		"	19	7^{35} A.M.	6488.1		6507.6		40.4	20.9
		"	19	9 A.M.	6551.1		6532.8		22.6	4.3
		"	19	11 A.M.	6656.1		6572.3		127.6	43.8
		"	19	2 P.M.	6752.3		6573.4		223.8	44.9
		"	19	4 P.M.	6647.2		6500.9		118.7	27.6
		"	19	9 P.M.	6417.8		6448.6		110.7	79.9
		"	20	7 A.M.	6485.3		6516.5		43.2	12.0
				Mean	6578.9		6528.5		117.4	40.7

Field Station.	Corresponding Station.	Date.			I.		II.		III.	IV.
					Uncorrected.	Range.	Corrected.	Range.	Uncorrected.	Corrected.
15 Gregory Flat.	Nevada City.	July 14	10²⁵ A.M.		4928.8		4879.5		140.0	90.7
		" 14	2 P.M.		4934.9		4804.0		146.1	15.2
		" 15	7 A.M.		4729.8		4752.6		59.0	36.2
		" 15	2 P.M.		4933.4		4802.5		144.6	13.7
		" 15	7 P.M.		4828.0		4813.5		39.2	24.7
		" 16	7 A.M.		4693.8		4716.3		95.0	72.5
		" 16	2 P.M.		4914.9		4784.5		126.1	4.3
		" 16	7 P.M.		4865.2		4850.6		76.4	61.8
		" 17	7 A.M.		4765.9		4788.7		22.9	0.1
		" 17	2 P.M.		4976.0		4844.0		187.2	55.2
		" 17	7 P.M.		4822.9		4808.4		34.1	19.6
		" 18	7¹⁵ A.M.		4797.9		4816.1		9.1	27.3
		" 18	2 P.M.		4911.6		4781.5		122.8	7.3
		" 18	7 P.M.		4836.5		4822.0		47.7	33.2
		" 19	7¹⁰ A.M.		4738.0		4756.2		50.8	32.6
		" 19	2 P.M.		4941.6	344.9	4810.6	226.2	152.8	21.8
		" 19	7 P.M.		4808.5		4794.1		19.7	5.3
		" 20	7 A.M.		4770.4		4793.2		18.4	4.4
		" 20	10 A.M.		4818.9		4783.9		30.1	4.9
		" 20	2 P.M.		4862.1		4733.3		73.3	55.5
		" 20	4 P.M.		4951.5		4842.6		162.7	53.8
		" 20	7 P.M.		4816.1		4801.7		27.3	12.9
		" 21	7 A.M.		4631.1		4653.3		157.7	135.5
		" 21	11 A.M.		4829.1		4768.3		40.3	20.5
		" 21	2 P.M.		4939.5		4808.5		150.7	19.7
		" 21	4 P.M.		4927.3		4819.0		138.5	30.2
		" 21	7 P.M.		4818.5		4804.0		29.7	15.2
		" 22	7 A.M.		4791.0		4818.0		2.2	29.2
		" 22	2 P.M.		4841.8		4713.5		53.0	75.3
		" 22	7 P.M.		4770.6		4756.3		18.2	32.5
		" 23	7 A.M.		4711.6		4734.1		77.2	54.7
			Mean		4835.7		4788.8		79.1	34.4
16 Camp 9.	Colfax.	Sept. 21	9 P.M.		1353.2		1369.6		22.1	5.7
		" 22	7 A.M.		1346.8		1361.4		28.5	13.9
		" 22	2 P.M.		1405.7		1371.8		30.4	3.5
		" 22	9 P.M.		1322.5		1338.6		52.8	36.7
		" 23	7 A.M.		1397.6		1412.7		22.3	37.4
		" 23	2 P.M.		1431.9		1397.2		56.6	21.9

Field Station.	Corresponding Station.	Date.			I. Uncorrected	Range.	II. Corrected.	Range.	III. Uncorrected.	IV. Corrected.
16 Camp 9 (Continued).	Colfax.	Sept.	23	9 P.M.	1365.5		1381.9		9.8	6.6
		"	24	7 A.M.	1369.8		1384.6		5.5	9.3
		"	24	2 P.M.	1397.5	109.4	1363.6	74.1	22.2	11.7
		"	24	9 P.M.	1365.9		1382.3		9.4	7.0
		"	25	7 A.M.	1366.8		1381.6		8.5	6.3
		"	25	2 P.M.	1389.9		1356.1		14.6	19.2
		"	25	9 P.M.	1353.9		1370.3		21.4	5.0
		"	26	7 A.M.	1355.6		1370.2		19.7	5.1
		"	26	2 P.M.	1389.2		1355.4		13.9	19.9
		"	26	9 P.M.	1390.8		1407.7		15.5	32.4
				Mean	1375.2		1375.3		22.1	15.1
17 Lakeport.	Sacramento	Oct.	19	7 A.M.	1247.3		1269.7		76.5	54.1
		"	19	2 P.M.	1353.5		1323.2		29.7	0.6
		"	19	9 P.M.	1231.2		1250.7		92.6	73.1
		"	20	7 A.M.	1237.5		1259.7		86.3	64.1
		"	20	2 P.M.	1369.9		1339.1		46.1	15.3
		"	20	9 P.M.	1249.3		1269.1		74.5	54.7
		"	21	7 A.M.	1259.8		1282.4		64.0	41.4
		"	21	2 P.M.	1386.9		1355.7		63.1	31.9
		"	21	9 P.M.	1321.3		1342.1		2.5	18.3
		"	22	7 A.M.	1316.1		1339.7		7.7	15.9
		"	22	2 P.M.	1386.3		1355.1		62.5	31.3
		"	23	7 A.M.	1333.1		1357.0		9.3	33.2
		"	23	2 P.M.	1332.7		1302.7		8.9	21.1
		"	23	9 P.M.	1287.0	183.2	1307.3	131.9	36.8	16.5
		"	24	7 A.M.	1264.5		1287.2		59.3	36.6
		"	24	2 P.M.	1414.4		1382.6		90.6	58.8
		"	24	9 P.M.	1346.7		1367.0		22.9	43.2
		"	25	7 A.M.	1313.8		1337.4		10.0	13.6
		"	25	2 P.M.	1402.3		1370.8		78.5	47.0
		"	25	9 P.M.	1325.5		1346.4		1.7	22.6
		"	26	7 A.M.	1297.4		1320.6		26.4	3.2
		"	26	2 P.M.	1354.9		1324.5		31.1	0.7
		"	26	9 P.M.	1336.6		1357.7		12.8	33.9
		"	27	7 A.M.	1282.5		1305.4		41.3	18.4
		"	27	2 P.M.	1407.2		1375.6		83.4	51.8
		"	27	9 P.M.	1270.8		1290.9		53.0	32.9
				Mean	1320.3		1323.8		45.1	32.1

Field Station.	Corresponding Station.	Date.			I. Uncorrected.	I. Range.	II. Corrected.	II. Range.	III. Uncorrected.	IV. Corrected.
18 Damascus.	Summit.	June	1	9 P.M.	2971.9		2984.7		57.2	44.4
		"	2	9 P.M.	3013.1		3026.0		16.0	3.1
		"	3	7 A.M.	3032.9	178.5	3042.0	107.1	3.8	12.9
		"	3	9 P.M.	3035.5		3048.5		6.4	19.4
		"	4	12 M.	3150.4		3090.2		121.3	61.1
		"	5	7¹⁵ A.M.	2977.1		2983.1		52.0	46.0
				Mean	3030.1		3029.1		42.8	31.1
19 Michigan Bluff	Colfax.	June	15	9 P.M.	1053.4		1057.9		9.9	5.4
		"	16	7 A.M.	1071.9		1075.1		8.6	11.8
		"	16	2 P.M.	1085.4		1056.2		22.1	7.1
		"	16	9 P.M.	1071.3		1075.9		8.0	12.6
		"	17	7 A.M.	1062.9		1066.1		0.4	2.8
		"	17	2 P.M.	1085.0		1055.8		21.7	7.5
		"	17	6³⁰ P.M.	1053.6		1045.9		9.7	17.4
		"	17	9 P.M.	1062.6		1067.0		0.7	3.7
		"	18	1³⁰ P.M.	1069.6		1041.6		6.3	21.7
		"	19	12⁴⁵ P.M.	1095.4	49.3	1069.1	46.1	32.1	5.8
		"	19	9 P.M.	1059.1		1063.6		4.2	0.3
		"	20	7 A.M.	1084.4		1087.7		21.1	24.4
		"	20	4¹⁵ P.M.	1063.6		1043.9		0.3	19.4
		"	20	9 P.M.	1061.8		1066.3		1.5	3.0
		"	21	7 A.M.	1056.7		1059.9		6.6	3.4
		"	21	2 P.M.	1097.0		1067.4		33.7	4.1
		"	21	9 P.M.	1047.7		1052.2		15.6	12.1
		"	22	8⁴⁵ A.M.	1080.4		1076.1		17.1	12.8
		"	22	9 P.M.	1070.3		1074.9		7.0	11.6
				Mean	1070.1		1063.3		11.9	9.8
20 Forest Hill.	Colfax.	June	26	7 A.M.	809.0		812.2		0.4	3.6
		"	26	2¹⁵ P.M.	823.9		801.8		15.3	6.8
		"	26	9 P.M.	777.7		781.2		30.9	27.4
		"	27	7²⁰ A.M.	803.4		805.5		5.2	3.1
		"	28	8 A.M.	811.8		811.8		3.2	3.2
		"	28	10¹⁵ A.M.	814.3		806.4		5.7	2.2
		"	28	12³⁰ P.M.	825.2		806.6		16.6	2.0
		"	28	7³⁰ P.M.	811.8		810.8		3.2	2.2
		"	28	9 P.M.	801.5		805.1		7.1	3.5

Field Station.	Corresponding Station.	Date.			I. Uncorrected.	Range.	II. Corrected.	Range.	III. Uncorrected.	IV. Corrected.
20 Forest Hill (*Continued*).	Colfax.	June	29	8³⁰ A.M.	811.3		809.7		2.7	1.1
		"	29	10³⁰ A.M.	818.9		809.9		10.3	1.3
		"	29	6⁴⁵ P.M.	823.1		818.9		14.5	10.3
		"	30	8³⁰ A.M.	802.5	69.0	801.0	43.5	6.1	7.6
		"	30	10 A.M.	816.1		809.2		7.5	0.6
		"	30	12 M.	826.4		809.9		17.8	1.3
		July	1	8⁴⁵ A.M.	816.7		813.6		8.1	5.0
		"	2	9¹⁵ A.M.	795.0		791.0		13.6	17.6
		"	3	8 A.M.	807.1		807.0		1.5	1.6
		"	4	9 A.M.	819.4		816.2		10.8	7.6
		"	6	9¹⁵ A.M.	828.5		824.4		19.9	15.8
		"	6	12 M.	839.3		822.5		30.7	13.9
		"	7	9 A.M.	827.9		824.7		19.3	16.1
		"	8	7 A.M.	803.8		807.0		4.8	1.6
		"	8	7 P.M.	796.0		793.1		12.6	15.5
		"	10	9¹⁰ A.M.	820.1		816.3		11.5	7.7
				Mean	813.2		808.6		11.2	7.1
21 Blacksmith Flat.	Georgetown	Sept.	15	4 P.M.	1195.5		1177.0		37.0	18.5
		"	15	6 P.M.	1154.7		1152.4		3.8	6.1
		"	15	9 P.M.	1135.4	60.1	1149.2	27.8	23.1	9.3
		"	16	8³⁰ A.M.	1156.3		1163.8		2.2	5.3
		"	16	5 P.M.	1161.1		1150.0		2.6	8.5
				Mean	1160.6		1158.5		17.7	9.5
22 Placerville.	Colfax.	Oct.	4	9 A.M.	545.3		551.3		14.3	8.3
		"	4	2 P.M.	575.7		565.2		16.1	5.6
		"	5	7 A.M.	559.6		571.5		0.0	11.9
		"	5	2 P.M.	579.8		569.3		20.2	9.7
		"	6	9 A.M.	585.4		591.8		25.8	32.2
		"	6	2 P.M.	588.7		578.2		29.1	18.6
		"	7	9³⁰ A.M.	566.5		570.9		6.9	11.3
		"	7	1 P.M.	571.3		561.8		11.7	2.2
		"	7	4 P.M.	568.1		562.8		8.5	3.2
		"	8	2 P.M.	556.6		546.5		3.0	13.1
		"	9	9³⁰ A.M.	549.6		553.6		10.0	6.0
		"	9	2 P.M.	575.2	53.7	564.7	50.9	15.6	5.1
		"	10	2 P.M.	556.7		546.6		2.9	13.0

Field Station.	Corresponding Station.	Date.			I. Uncorrected.	Range.	II. Corrected.	Range.	III. Uncorrected.	IV. Corrected.
22 Placerville (*Continued.*)	Colfax.	Oct.	11	9³⁰ A.M.	548.7		552.7		10.9	6.9
		"	11	2 P.M.	571.6		561.1		12.0	1.5
		"	13	9 A.M.	538.4		544.3		21.2	15.3
		"	13	3 P.M.	559.3		550.9		0.3	8.7
		"	14	2 P.M.	562.0		551.8		2.4	7.8
		"	16	2 P.M.	557.4		546.3		2.2	13.3
		"	17	9 A.M.	535.0		540.9		24.6	18.7
		"	20	2 P.M.	571.5		561.0		11.9	1.4
		"	21	9 A.M.	562.8		568.8		3.2	9.2
		"	21	1 P.M.	573.0		563.5		13.4	3.9
				Mean	563.4		559.6		11.6	9.9
23 Geyser Springs	Colfax.	Sept.	15	9 P.M.	981.0		993.0		19.3	31.3
		"	16	7 A.M.	975.1		985.7		13.4	24.0
		"	16	2 P.M.	947.4	46.2	924.4	80.8	14.3	37.3
		"	17	7 A.M.	960.4		970.7		1.3	9.0
		"	17	2 P.M.	934.8		912.2		26.9	49.5
		"	17	9 P.M.	972.3		984.1		10.6	22.4
				Mean	961.8		961.7		14.3	28.9
24 Long Valley.	Colfax.	Nov.	8	7 A.M.	1046.7		1062.9		21.7	5.5
		"	8	2 P.M.	1050.6		1034.0		17.6	34.4
		"	9	2 P.M.	1039.0		1022.6		29.4	45.8
		"	9	9 P.M.	1092.8	53.8	1106.9	84.3	24.4	38.5
		"	13	7 A.M.	1075.4		1091.9		7.0	23.5
		"	13	2 P.M.	1071.7		1054.9		3.3	13.5
		"	13	9 P.M.	1089.6		1103.7		21.2	35.3
					1066.5		1068.4		17.8	28.1

The cases cited as illustrations have been selected mainly from those where a large number of independent computations have been made, for it is from the study of such cases in particular that the real worth of the new tables can be determined most satisfactorily. They have also been chosen with the view of illustrating the use of the tables under a considerable variety of conditions, some acquaintance with which, as well as with the geographical positions or other peculiarities of the stations, will be necessary for the complete understanding of the significance of each case, and for estimating its relative importance compared with the others. The geographical relations of Sacramento, Colfax, and Summit have been described in a previous chapter (pages 29 and 30). Of the other points used as corresponding stations, Nevada City and Georgetown are practically the equivalent of Colfax, the former being about twelve, and the latter about fifteen miles distant, with a difference of altitude not exceeding 250 feet; Smartsville lies in the foot-hills of Yuba county, at an altitude of 762 feet above the sea, and about twenty miles to the northwest of the line joining Sacramento and Colfax; Dutch Flat is a station on the Central Pacific Railroad, thirteen miles above Colfax; the barometer hung in the banking-office of Messrs. W. & P. Nicholls, at a point 728 feet above the barometer at Colfax.

The positions of the field-stations and their distances, in direct lines, from the corresponding stations are approximately as follows: —

1. Riley Lane's is in the valley of the Sacramento river, a few miles below Smartsville.

2. Tompkins's is at the head-waters of the Yuba river, thirty-four miles from Smartsville.

3. Blue Cañon is a station on the Central Pacific Railroad, about twenty miles from Summit.

4 and 5. Murphy's and Columbia are about eighty-five miles nearly due south from Summit, and do not differ more than 300 feet in altitude from Colfax.

6, 8, and 9. The positions of Dutch Flat and Nevada City are described above.

7. Gold Run is a station on the Central Pacific Railroad ten miles above Colfax.

10. You Bet is in Nevada county, eight miles from Colfax.

11 and 12. Lone Pine and Bend City are in Owen's Valley, on the east side of the Sierra Nevada mountains, and nearly two hundred and fifty miles from Smartsville.

13, 14, and 15. Camp 37 and Gregory Flat are both on the eastern slope of the Sierra Nevada mountains; the former is about one hundred and eighty miles, the latter one hundred and fifty, southeast of Smartsville.

16. Camp 9 is about ten miles south of Clear Lake, and ninety miles from Colfax.

17. Lakeport lies on Clear Lake, eighty miles from Sacramento.

18. Damascus is in Placer county, about thirty miles from Summit.

19 and 20. Michigan Bluff and Forest Hill are in Placer county, not more than twelve miles from Colfax.

21. Blacksmith Flat is in El Dorado county, a few miles only from Georgetown.

22. Placerville is in El Dorado county, about twenty-seven miles southerly from Colfax.

23 and 24. Geyser Springs and Long Valley are both in the region visited by the Clear Lake party.

An inspection of the preceding table will show that in all but the last two cases the average errors of the corrected results (the means in column IV.) are less than those of the uncorrected results (column III.); and that in only a little more than one quarter of the individual computations (115 out of 402, or twenty-eight per cent) has the error of the uncorrected results been increased by the application of the correction. Among the whole number of cases from which those in the tables have been selected, one hundred and seventy-one in all, there are only thirty in which the application of the corrections has increased the average error, and of these only five can properly be called bad cases. Two of these five are given in the table (Nos. 23 and 24). Taking all the one hundred and seventy-one cases together, involving as they do eleven hundred and ninety-nine separate computations, there are three hundred and seventy-eight (or thirty-one and six tenths per cent) instances where the use of the new tables has resulted in an increase of the error, although in the most of the instances the increase has been slight. This is a large percentage, it is true, but perhaps no larger than might be expected, when all the adverse conditions are taken into consideration.

If it be objected that there is no sufficient justification for taking the means of the corrected results (column II.) as the closest attainable approximations to the real differences of altitude between the stations, and that by so doing the errors of the corrected results (column IV.) may have been made to appear less than they otherwise would, the reply is, that, even if the means of the uncorrected results (column I.) had been assumed to be the true differences of altitude, it would not have affected to any material extent the conclusions to be drawn from the study of columns III. and IV. as they now stand. In all the cases cited in the table, excepting Nos. 3, 8, 13, 14, and 15, there is a remarkably close agreement between the mean values of the uncorrected and the corrected results. This shows that the mean result obtained from a considerable series of barometric observations, especially when the observations are taken at different hours of the day and extend over several days, may not be far from the truth, notwithstanding the wide variations of the separate computations from the mean value, but does not establish any further presumption in favor of its accuracy.* The preponderance of evidence, derived from all sources, is decidedly in favor of the mean of the corrected results.

The question now arises, what conclusion can be drawn from the results in these one hundred and seventy-one cases as to the advantage gained by using the new tables? The most satisfactory way of meeting this question seems to be to ascertain the average error for a thousand feet of difference of altitude, before and after the application of the corrections. The aggregate of all the differences of level in the twenty-four cases cited in the table is 54,772 feet. The aggregates of the average errors in columns III. and IV. are 929.8 and 527.7 feet. This makes the average errors per thousand feet 16.97 and 9.63 feet respectively. The aggregate of the differences of level in the one hundred and seventy-one cases taken together is 279,592.6 feet, and of the average errors, 4,838.0 and 2,742.1 feet. This makes the average errors per thousand feet 17.30 and 9.81 feet.

The conclusion, therefore, is that, roughly speaking, *the residual errors of the computations based upon the old tables alone are reduced about one half by the use of the new tables,* — a conclusion identical with that reached on page 96, as the result of the examination of one hundred and forty-six different cases.

---

* According to the tables given on pages 87 and 88, the mean of the day is, for certain months in the year, almost exactly the same as the mean of the year. For instance, in table XXIV., the correction to be applied for each thousand feet from sea-level to seven thousand feet is, in June, − 1.9 ; in July, + 1.0 ; in August, + 2.6.

Printed in Dunstable, United Kingdom

82202511R00071